CW01217715

I have edited Clive Gilson's books for over a decade now – he's prolific and can turn his hand to many genres. poetry, short fiction, contemporary novels, folklore, and science fiction – and the common theme is that none of them ever fails to take my breath away. There's something in each story that is either memorably poignant, hauntingly unnerving, or sidesplittingly funny.

Lorna Howarth, *The Write Factor*

Tales From The World's Firesides is a grand project. I've collected '000's of traditional texts as part of other projects, and while many of the original texts are available through channels like Project Gutenberg, some of the narratives can be hard to read by modern readers, and so the Fireside project was born. Put simply, I collect, collate and adapt traditional tales from around the world and publish them as a modern archive. This collection, *Dog Tails*, collects a host of stories from around the world, all of them with one thing in common; they tell the story of dogs and their many wonderful adventures. These collections are born out of my love of storytelling and I hope that you'll share my affection for traditional doggy tales, myths and legends.

Chapter image by Gordon Johnson, Pixabay
Cover image by Clive Gilson

DOG TAILS

Traditional tales, fables and legends from around the world about our canine friends ...

Compiled, Adapted & Edited by Clive Gilson

Tales from the World's Firesides

Dog Tails, edited by Clive Gilson, Solitude, Bath, UK

www.clivegilson.com

First published in 2024

All rights reserved. No portion of this book may be reproduced in any form without permission from the publisher, except as permitted by United Kingdom copyright law.

This is a work of fiction. Names, characters, places, and incidents either are the products of the author's imagination or are used fictitiously. Any resemblance to actual persons, living or dead, businesses, companies, events, or locales is entirely coincidental.

Printed by IngramSpark

ISBN: 978-1-915081-09-4

CONTENTS

Preface
A Cruel Man and a Fairy Dog
Dog, And His Human Speech
A Witch In The Shape Of A Dog.
How The Dog Came To Live With Man
Concerning Dogs
Bran, The Wolf Dog.
Concerning Bran
The Coin-Sith
The Dog and His Shadow
The Three Black Dogs
The Dog and the Crocodile
The Dog And The Root Digger
The Dog in the Manger
The Golden Beetle Or Why The Dog Hates The Cat
Dog Mouths
The Moddey Doo Or The Black Dog Of Peel Castle
Cwn Annwn
The Dog of Montargis
Dogs Over The Water
The Dog Who Was A Rajah
Grateful Dogs
Mary, Queen Of Scots
The Russet Dog
The Farmer and His Dog
Why Dog And Cat Are Enemies
Still Waters Run Deep; Or The Dancing Dog
The Story Of The Dog And The Snake And The Cure Of Headache
Story of the Buddhist monk who was bitten by a dog.
Anubis, The Dog Headed God
The Black Dog And The Thumbless Hand
Hog And Dog

The Boy Who Was Changed into a Dog.

The Dog And The Cock

The Dog And The Dog Dealer

The Dog And The Moon

The Dog And The Sparrow

The Dog Fanti

Macphie's Black Dog

The Dog O' Mause

Why Dogs Sniff

The Dog's Trial

The Black Dogs

The Guilty Dogs

The Legend Of Artemis

The Man And The Water-Dogs

Church Grim

The Orphan Boy And The Hell-Hounds

The Old Dog

The Owl And Lamp, And The Dogs And The Ragman

The Ass And The Little Dog

The Story Of The Partridge, The Fox And The Hound

The Lame Dog

The Three Dogs

Dog And His False Friend Leopard

The Dog Gellert

Cerberus

Mr. Fox's Housewarming

Ned Dog And Billy Goat

The Origin Of The Dog

Dog And Repo

Where The Sparks Go

Black Shuck

Dog And The Kingship

The Youth And The Dog-Dance

The Story Of Kitinda And Her Wise Dog

The Dog Bride

The Dog And The Corpse

The Giant Dog

The Barghest

The Strange Tale Of Doctor Dog

A Brave Dog

Parson Puss And Parson Dog

How The Dog Outwitted The Leopard

The Wolf And The Dog

Gytrash

The Little Hunting Dog

The Elephant And The Dog

Why Dogs Wag their Tails

Why Mr. Dog Runs Brother Rabbit

Kulloo, A Faithful Dog

The Bear, The Dog, And The Cat

Why Dogs Chase Foxes

The Dog And The Shadow

Black Dog Of The Pennine Hills

Why A Man Loves His Dog

The Three Friends, - The Monkey, the Dog, and the Carabao

The First Lapdog

The Word Hound

About the Editor

Preface

I've been collecting and telling stories for a couple of decades now, having had several of my own fictional works published in recent years. My particular focus is on short story writing in the realms of magical realities and science fiction fantasies.

I've always drawn heavily on traditional folk and fairy tales, and in so doing have amassed a collection of many thousands of these tales from around the world. It has been one of my long-standing ambitions to gather these stories together and to create a library of tales that tell the stories of places and peoples from the four corners of our world.

One of the main motivations for me in undertaking the project is to collect and tell stories that otherwise might be lost or, at best forgotten. Given that a lot of my sources are from early collectors, particularly covering works produced in the late eighteenth century, throughout the nineteenth century, and in the early years of the twentieth century, I do make every effort to adapt stories for a modern reader. Early collectors had a different world view to many of us today, and often expressed views about race and gender, for example, that we find difficult to reconcile in the early years of the twenty-first century. I try, although with varying degrees of success, to update these stories with sensitivity while trying to stay as true to the original spirit of each story as I can.

I also want to assure readers that I try hard not to comment on or appropriate originating cultures. It is almost certainly true that the early collectors of these tales, with their then prevalent world views, have made assumptions about the originating cultures that have given us these tales. I hope that you'll accept my mission to preserve these tales, however and wherever I find them, as just that. I have, therefore, made sure that every story has a full attribution, covering both the original collector / writer and the collection title that this version has been adapted from, as well as having notes about publishers and other relevant and, I hope, interesting source data. Wherever possible I have added a cultural or indigenous attribution, although for some of the tiles, the country-based theme is obvious.

This volume, *Dog Tails*, is a collection of tales from around the world where our canine friends take centre stage. Apart from the obvious love that we have for dogs (we have two rescued greyhounds in our family), I think that there are a number of compelling reasons for putting this small collection together.

Dogs are widely recognized and loved animals across different cultures and societies. Including them in folk tales makes these stories relatable to people from various backgrounds.

As we would probably expect, dogs are often portrayed as loyal and faithful companions in folk tales, emphasizing their valued role as friends and protectors. Of course, no folk tale tradition would be complete without its darker tales too, but overall I think these tales celebrate the special bond between humans and dogs, appealing to our emotional connection with these animals.

Many folk tales featuring dogs convey moral lessons or teach virtues such as loyalty, bravery, and kindness. Through the trials and adventures faced by dog characters, these stories impart wisdom and guidance to listeners, often in a way that is accessible and engaging, especially for children.

Like all folk tales and fairy tales, those featuring dogs offer a form of entertainment and escapism. They transport listeners to fantastical worlds where animals speak, magical events occur, and challenges are overcome, providing a temporary escape from reality.

Many folk tales featuring dogs are part of a culture's rich oral tradition, passed down through generations. By preserving and sharing these stories, we not only celebrate cultural heritage but also gain insight into the values, beliefs, and customs of different societies and their relationships with our canine friends.

Overall, I believe that folk tales and fairy tales featuring dogs resonate with audiences because they speak to universal themes, celebrate the human-animal bond, and offer valuable insights and entertainment for people of all ages.

There is a great gift given to each of us through storytelling. Since the first of our ancestors sat around in a cave, contemplating an ape's place in the world, we have, as a species, told each other stories of magic and cunning and caution and love. When I began to research tales from the Celts, tales from Indonesia, tales from Africa and the Far East, tales from everywhere, one of the things that struck me clearly was just how similar are our roots. We share characters and characteristics. The nature of these tales is so similar underneath the local camouflage. Human beings clearly share a storytelling heritage so much deeper than the world that we see superficially as always having been just as it is now.

These tales were originally told by firelight as a way of preserving histories and educating both adult and child. These tales form part of our shared heritage, witches, warts, fantastic beasts, and all. They can be dark and violent. They can be sweet and loving. They are we and we are they in so many ways. I've loved researching and reading these stories. I hope you do too.

Clive

Bath 2024

A Cruel Man and a Fairy Dog

A Welsh Tale

This tale is adapted from Elias Owen's book Welsh Folk-Lore: A Collection of the Folk-Tales and Legends of North Wales, which is a significant work in the field of folkloristics, focusing on the rich oral traditions of North Wales. Published by Elliot Stock of London in 1896, the book is a comprehensive compilation of the myths, legends, and folk-tales that Owen meticulously gathered from various sources, including oral testimonies and older manuscripts.

A Fairy dog lost its master and wandered about here and there seeking him. A farmer saw the dog, and took it home with him, but he behaved very unkindly towards the wee thing, and gave it little to eat, and shouted at it, and altogether he showed a hard heart.

One evening a little old man called at this farmer's house, and inquired if any stray dog was there. He gave a few particulars respecting the dog, and mentioned the day that it had been lost.

The farmer answered in the affirmative, and the stranger said that the dog was his, and asked the farmer to give it up to him. This the farmer willingly did, for he placed no value on the dog.

The little man was very glad to get possession of his lost dog, and on departing he placed a well filled purse in the farmer's hand. Sometime afterwards the farmer looked into the purse, intending to take a coin out of it, when to his surprise and annoyance he found therein nothing but leaves.

The farmer got what he deserved, for he had been very cruel to the wee dog.

Dog, And His Human Speech

An African Tale

This story has been edited and adapted from Robert Hamill Nassau's Where Animals Talk, first published in 1912 by Richard G. Badger at The Gorham Press, based out of Boston. This tale was originally told by storytellers from the Benga tribe.

Dog and his mother were the only inhabitants of their hamlet. He had the power to speak both as a beast and as a human being.

One day the mother said to the son, "You are now a strong man. Go, and seek a marriage. Go, and marry Eyâle, the daughter of Njambo."

And he said to his mother, "I will go tomorrow."

That day darkened. And they both went to lie down in their places for sleep. Then soon, another day began to break.

Dog said to his mother, "This is the time of my journey."

It was about sun-rise in the morning. And he began his journey. He went the distance of about eight miles, and arrived at the journey's end before the middle of the morning.

He entered the house of Njambo, the father of Eyâle. Njambo and his wife saluted him, "Mbolo!" and he responded, "Ai! mbolo!" Njambo asked him, "My friend! What is the cause of your journey?"

Dog, with his animal language, answered, "I have come to marry your daughter Eyâle."

Njambo consented, and the mother of the girl also agreed. They called their daughter, and asked her, and she also replied, "Yes! with all my heart." This young woman was of very fine appearance in face and body. So, all the parties agreed to the marriage.

In the evening, when they sat down at supper, the son-in-law, Dog, was not able to eat for some unknown reason. Then the day darkened, and they went to their sleep.

And, then, daylight broke. But, by an hour after sunrise in the morning, Dog had not risen, for he was still asleep.

The mother of the woman said to her, "Get some water ready for the washing of your husband's face, whenever he shall awake." She also said to her daughter, "I am going to go into the forest to the plantation to get food for your husband, for, since his coming, he has not eaten. Also, here is a chicken. The lads may kill and prepare it. But, you yourself must split ngândâ gourd-seeds to mash into a pudding."

She handed Eyâle the dish of gourd-seeds, and went off into the forest. Njambo also went away on an errand with his wife. The daughter took the dish of seeds, and, sitting down, began to shell them. As she shelled the seeds, she threw the kernels on the ground, but the shells she put on a plate.

Shortly after the mother had gone, Dog woke from sleep. He rose from his bed, and came out to the room where his wife was, and stood near her, watching her working at the seeds. He stood silent, looking closely, and observed that she was still throwing away the kernels, the good part, and saving the shells on the plate. He spoke to her with his human voice, "No, woman, not so! Why do you throw the good parts to the ground, and keep the worthless husks on the plate?"

While he was speaking to his wife, she suddenly fell to the ground. And at once she died. He laid hold of her to lift her up. But, she was a corpse.

Soon afterwards, the father and the mother came, having returned from their errands. They found their child a corpse, and they said to Dog, "Mbwa! What is this?"

He, with his own language replied, "I cannot tell."

But, they insisted, "Tell us the reason!"

So Dog spoke with his human voice, "You went to the forest while I was asleep. You, Man, you also went in company with your wife, while I was asleep. When I rose from sleep, I found my wife was cracking ngândâ. She was taking the good kernels to throw on the ground, and was keeping the shells for the plate. And I spoke and told her, 'The good kernels which you are throwing on the ground are to be eaten, not the husks.'"

While he was telling them this, they too, also fell to the ground, and died, apparently without cause.

When the people of the town heard about all this, they said, "This person carries an evil Medicine for killing people. Let him be seized and killed!"

So Dog fled away rapidly into the forest, and he finally reached the hamlet where his mother lived. His body was scratched and torn by the branches and thorns of the bushes of the forest during his hasty flight. His mother exclaimed, "Mbwa! What's the matter? Such haste! And your body so disordered!"

He replied, using their own language, "No! I won't tell you. I won't speak."

But, his mother begged him, "Please, my child, tell me!"

So, finally, he spoke, using his strange voice, and said, "My mother, I tell you, Njambo and his wife liked me for the marriage, and the woman consented entirely. I was asleep when the Man and his wife went to the forest. When I rose from my sleep, I found the woman Eyâle cracking ngândâ, and throwing away the kernels, and keeping the husks. And I told her, 'The good ones which you are throwing away are the ones to be eaten.' And, at once she died."

While he was speaking to his mother, she also fell dead on the ground. The news was carried to the town of Dog's mother's brother, and very many people came to the Mourning. His Uncle came to Dog, and said, "Mbwa! What is the reason of all this?"

But Dog would not answer. He only said, "No! I won't speak." Then they all begged him, "Tell us the reason."

But he replied only, "No! I won't speak."

Finally, as they urged him, he chose two of them, and said to the company, "The rest of you remain here, and watch while I go and speak to these two."

Then Dog spoke to those two men with the same voice as he had to his mother. And, at once they died, just as she had died. Then he exclaimed, "Ah! No! If I speak so, people will come to an end!"

And all the people agreed, "Yes, Mbwa! It is so. Your human speech kills us people. Don't speak any more."

And he went away to live with Mankind but has never spoken the words of man since.

A Witch In The Shape Of A Dog.

An Iroquois Tale

This tale has been adapted from Erminnie A. Smith's book Myths of the Iroquois, which is a notable work in the field of ethnology and Native American studies. Published in 1883 by the Smithsonian Institution's Bureau of Ethnology, this book is a significant collection of the myths and legends of the Iroquois people, providing valuable insights into their culture, beliefs, and oral traditions.

Witches could and did assume animal shapes. On the Buffalo Reservation a man saw a "witch-woman" coming, with fire streaming from her mouth. Crossing a creek and obtaining his gun the man returned and saw a dog at no great distance resting its forefeet upon a log, and it had fire streaming from its mouth and nostrils. The man fired at it and saw it fall, but as it was very dark he dared not go near it

On the following morning he went to the spot and saw where it had fallen, by the marks of blood from its wound. Tracking it by this means he followed its path until it had reached a bridge, where the woman's tracks took the place of the dog's tracks in the path. He followed the bloody trail to the Tonawanda Reservation, where he found the woman. She had died from the effect of the shot.

How The Dog Came To Live With Man

A Tale From the Khasis - India

This story has been edited and adapted from K. U. Rafy's Folk-Tales of the Khasis, first published in 1920 by MacMillan and Company, London & Canada.

In the happy olden days, when the animals lived together at peace in the forest, they used to hold fairs and markets after the manner of mankind. The most important fair of all was called "Ka Iew Luri Lura" (the Fair of Luri Lura), which was held at stated intervals in the Bhoi (forest) country. All the animals gathered there, each one bringing some article of merchandise, according to the decree which demanded that every animal that came to the fair should bring something to sell. No matter whether he was young or old, rich or poor, no one was to come empty-handed, for they wanted to enhance the popularity of the market. U Khla, the tiger, was appointed governor of the fair.

Man was excluded from these fairs as he was looked upon as an enemy. He used to hunt the animals with his bow and arrows, so they had ceased to fraternise with him and kept out of his way. But one day the dog left his own kindred in the jungle, and became the attendant of Man. The following story tells how that came to pass.

One day U Ksew, the dog, walked abroad in search of goods to sell at the fair. The other animals were thrifty and industrious, they worked to produce their merchandise, but the dog, being of an indolent nature, did not like to work, though he was very keen to go to the fair. So, to avoid the censure of his neighbours and the punishment of the governor of the fair, he set out in search of something he could get without much labour to himself. He trudged about the country all day, inquiring at many villages, but when evening-time came he had not succeeded in purchasing any suitable goods, and he began to fear that he would have to forgo the pleasure of attending the fair after all.

Just as the sun was setting he found himself on the outskirts of Saddew village, on the slopes of the Shillong Mountain, and as he sniffed the air he became aware of a strong and peculiar odour, which he guessed came from some cooked food. Being hungry after his long tramp, he pushed his way forward, following the scent till he came to a house right in the middle of the village, where he saw the family at dinner, which he noticed they were eating with evident relish. The dinner consisted of fermented Khasi beans, known as ktung rymbai, from which the strong smell emanated.

The Khasis are naturally a very cordial and hospitable people, and when the good wife of the house saw the dog standing outside looking wistfully at them she invited him to partake of what food there was left in the pot. U Ksew thankfully accepted, and by reason of his great hunger he ate heartily, regardless of the strange flavour and smell of the food, and he considered the ktung rymbai very palatable.

It dawned on him that here, quite by accident, he had found a novel and marketable produce to take to the fair, and it happened that the kindly family who had entertained him had a quantity of the stuff for sale which they kept in earthen jars, sealed with clay to retain its flavour. After a little palaver according to custom, a bargain was struck, and U Ksew became the owner of one good-sized jar of ktung rymbai, which he cheerfully took on his back. He made his way across the hills to Luri Lura fair, chuckling to himself as he anticipated the sensation he would create and the profits he would gain, and the praise he would win for being so enterprising.

On the way he encountered many of the animals who like himself were all going to Luri Lura, and carrying merchandise on their backs to sell at the fair. To them U Ksew boasted of the wonderful food he had discovered and was bringing with him to the market in the earthen jar under the clay seal. He talked so much about it that the contents of the earthen jar became the general topic of conversation between the animals, for never had such an article been known at Luri Lura.

When he arrived at the fair the dog walked in with great consequence, and installed himself and his earthen jar in the most central place with much clatter and ostentation. Then he began to shout at the top of his voice, "Come and buy my good food," and what with his boastings on the road and the noise he made at the fair, a very large company gathered round him, stretching their necks to have a glimpse at the strange-looking jar, and burning with curiosity to see the much-advertised contents.

U Ksew, with great importance, proceeded to uncover the jar, but as soon as he broke the clay seal a puff of the most unsavoury and foetid odour issued forth and drove all the animals scrambling to a safe distance, much to the dog's discomfiture and the merriment of the crowd. They hooted and jeered, and made all sorts of disparaging remarks till U Ksew felt himself covered with shame.

The stag pushed forward, and to show his disdain he contemptuously kicked the earthen jar till it broke. This increased the laughter and the jeering, and more of the animals came forward, and they began to trample the ktung rymbai in the mud, taking no notice of the protestations of U Ksew, who felt himself very unjustly treated. He went to U Khla, the governor of the fair, to ask for redress, but here again he was met with ridicule and scorn, and told that he deserved all the treatment he had received for filling the market-place with such a stench.

At last U Ksew's patience wore out, he grew snappish and angry, and with loud barks and snarls he began to curse the animals with many curses, threatening to be avenged upon them all someday. At the time no one heeded his curses and threats, for the dog was but a contemptible animal in their estimation, and it was not thought possible for him to work much harm. Yet even on that day a part of his curse came true, for the animals found to their dismay that the smell of the ktung rymbai clung to their paws and their hoofs, and could not be obliterated, so the laughter was not all on their side.

Humiliated and angry, the dog determined to leave the fair and the forest and his own tribe, and to seek more congenial surroundings. so he went away from Luri Lura, never to return, and came once more to Saddew village, to the house of the family from whom he had bought the offending food. When the master of the house heard the story of the ill-treatment he had suffered from the animals, he pitied U Ksew, and he also considered that the insults touched himself as well as the dog, inasmuch as it was he who had prepared and sold the ktung rymbai. So he spoke consolingly to U Ksew and patted his head and told him to remain in the village with him, and that he would protect him and help him to avenge his wrongs upon the animals.

After the coming of the dog, Man became a very successful hunter, for the dog, who always accompanied him when he went out to hunt, was able to follow the trail of the animals by the smell of the ktung rymbai, which adhered to their feet. Thus the animals lived to rue the day when they played their foolish pranks on U Ksew and his earthen jar at the fair of Luri Lura.

Man, having other occupations, could not always go abroad to the jungle to hunt. so in order to secure a supply of meat for himself during the non-hunting seasons he tamed pigs and kept them at hand in the village. When the dog came he shared the dwelling and the meals of the pig, U Sniang; they spent their days in idleness, living on the bounty of Man.

One evening, as Man was returning from his field, tired with the day's toil, he noticed the two idle animals and he said to himself--"It is very foolish of me to do all the hard work myself while these two well-fed creatures are lying idle. They ought to take a turn at doing some work for their food."

The following morning Man commanded the two animals to go to the field to plough in his stead. When they arrived there U Sniang, in obedience to his master's orders, began to dig with his snout, and by nightfall had managed to furrow quite a large patch of the field, but U Ksew, according to his indolent habits, did no work at all. He lay in the shade all day, or amused himself by snapping at the flies. In the evening, when it was time to go home, he would start running backwards and forwards over the furrows, much to the annoyance of the pig.

The same thing happened for many days in succession, till the patience of the pig was exhausted, and on their return from the field one evening he went and informed their master of the conduct of the dog, how he was idling the whole day and leaving all the work for him to do.

The master was loth to believe these charges against U Ksew, whom he had found such an active and willing helper in the chase: he therefore determined to go and examine the field. When he came there he found only a few of the footprints of the pig, while those of the dog were all over the furrows. He at once concluded that U Sniang had falsely charged his friend, and he was exceedingly wroth with him.

When he came home, Man called the two animals to him, and he spoke very angrily to U Sniang, and told him that henceforth he would have to live in a little sty by himself, and to eat only the refuse from Man's table and other common food, as a punishment for making false charges against his friend, but the dog would be privileged to live in the house with his master, and to share the food of his master's family.

Thus it was that the dog came to live with Man.

Concerning Dogs

An Irish Tale

This tale has been adapted from Jane Francesca Agnes Wilde's book, Ancient legends, Mystic Charms & Superstitions of Ireland, published by Chatto And Windus, London in 1919.

Some very weird superstitions exist in Ireland concerning the howlings of dogs. If a dog is heard to howl near the house of a sick person, all hope of his recovery is given up, and the patient himself sinks into despair, knowing that his doom is sealed. But the Irish are not alone in holding this superstition. The Egyptians, Hebrews, Greeks, and Romans all looked on the howling of the dog as ominous. The very word howling may be traced in the Latin *ululu*, the Greek *holuluzo*, the Hebrew *hululue*, and the Irish *ulluloo*.

In Ireland the cry raised at the funeral ceremony was called the *Caoin*, or keen, probably from χυων, a dog. And this doleful lamentation was also common to other nations of antiquity. The Hebrews, Greeks, and Romans had their hired mourners, who, with dishevelled hair and mournful cadenced hymns, led on the melancholy parade of death. Thus the Trojan women keened over Hector, the chorus being led by the beautiful Helen herself.

The howling of the dog was considered by these nations as the first note of the funeral dirge and the signal that the coming of death was near.

But the origin of the superstition may be traced back to Egypt, where dogs and dog-faced gods were objects of worship; probably because Sirius, the Dog-star, appeared precisely before the rising of the Nile, and thereby gave the people a mystic and supernatural warning to prepare for the overflow.

The Romans held that the howling of dogs was a fatal presage of evil, and it is noted amongst the direful omens that preceded the death of Cæsar. Horace also says that Canidia by her spells and sorceries could bring ghosts of dogs from hell; and Virgil makes the dog to howl at the approach of Hecate.

It is remarkable that when dogs see spirits (and they are keenly sensitive to spirit influence) they never bark, but only howl. The Rabbins say that "when the Angel of Death enters a city the dogs do howl. But when Elias appears then the dogs rejoice and are merry." And Rabbi Jehuda the Just states, that once upon a time when the Angel of Death entered a house the dog howled and fled; but being presently brought back he lay down in fear and trembling, and so died.

This strange superstition concerning the howling of dogs, when, as is supposed, they are conscious of the approach of the Spirit of Death, and see him though he is shrouded and invisible to human eyes, may be found pervading the legends of all nations from the earliest period down to the present time; for it still exists in full force amongst all classes, the educated, as well as the unlettered, and to this day the howling of a dog where a sick person is lying is regarded in Ireland in all grades of society with pale dismay as a certain sign of approaching death.

The Irish may have obtained the superstition through Egypt, Phœnicia, or Greece, for it is the opinion of some erudite writers that the Irish wolf-dog (*Canis gracius Hibernicus*) was descended from the dogs of Greece.

It is strange and noteworthy that although the dog is so faithful to man, yet it is never mentioned in the Bible without an expression of contempt, and Moses in his code of laws makes the dog an unclean animal, probably to deter the Israelites from the Egyptian worship of this animal. It was the lowest term of offence. "Is thy servant a dog?" False teachers, persecutors, Gentiles, unholy men, and others sunk in sin and vileness were called dogs, while at the same time the strange prophetic power of these animals was universally acknowledged and recognized.

The Romans sacrificed a dog at the Lupercalia in February. And to meet a dog with her whelps was considered in the highest degree unlucky. Of all living creatures the name of "dog" applied to anyone expressed the lowest form of insult, contempt, and reproach. Yet, of all animals, the dog has the noblest qualities, the highest intelligence, and the most enduring affection for man.

Dog Tails – Canine Fairy Tales, Myths And Legends

Bran, The Wolf Dog.

An Irish Tale

This tale is adapted from the book, Stories of Enchantment, which is a book written by Jane Pentzer Myers and published by A. C. McClurg and Co. in Chicago in 1901. This book is a collection of fairy tales and stories meant to captivate and enchant readers, primarily children. The tales are likely imbued with the elements typical of early 20th-century fairy tales, such as magical creatures, moral lessons, and fantastical adventures.

On a high cliff overlooking the ocean, on the western coast of Ireland, stand the ruins of an old castle. The short grass grows on the floor of the great hall, and the wind sighs and howls through its broken walls, with a sound half human, half animal.

For generations the local people have named it "The Wolf's Castle." Even long years ago, when it was tenanted by kindly folk and was running over with life and happiness, it had already earned its grim name.

Max had been out hunting. He had spent the day in the woods and fields, and now as night fell, dark and lowering, he hastened his steps. The first scattering drops of rain struck his face, and the wind was rising. It moaned and howled like the distant cry of a wolf; it made Max feel strangely nervous and frightened.

"Frightened!", he laughed at the thought. "A boy of twelve frightened by the wind!"

And yet, listen! The patter of the rain (coming faster now) sounds on the leaves like the stealthy tread of some animal.

"If it is a wolf, it is the ghost of one, for there are no wolves in this country now," thought Max. "How like a sigh from human lips the wind sounds!"

*

"Home at last, I am thankful to say," and Max ran swiftly round to the back door. As he closed it, the wind gave a long-drawn wail, and he almost fancied a hand strove to draw him back into the darkness.

"I think I need my supper," thought he. "Hunger makes a fellow light-headed."

Entering the kitchen with exultant heart but studied indifference, he threw his game down on the table before the admiring cook, and then hastened to change his clothes. Soon, over a good supper, he had forgotten the uncanny night outside, though the wind still howled and the rain beat against the window.

After supper Max went into the library. How cosy and comfortable it was, with a fire in the grate, an easy-chair drawn in front of it, and the shadows dancing over books and pictures!

"I'll sit here in front of the fire and rest," thought he. He sat there mentally reviewing the day's sport. "I need a good dog," he said. "I must have one." He paused and looked around the room. "Why, what is that?" he asked himself, for there, lying in front of the fire, basking in the heat, was an immense dog, with shaggy coat and pointed ears.

Max called to him, "Here, old fellow; here, Bran, for he seemed to know the dog's name. "How did I come to know it, I wonder!" thought Max, for at the first call, the dog had raised his head and beat his great tail upon the floor. At the mention of his name he sprang to his feet, and came crouching and trembling with joy to lick the hands and shoes of the lad.

"What is it then, good dog? Tell me your story, for I'm sure you have one to tell," coaxed Max.

Did he tell it, or did Max dream? For as the dog rested his head on the boy's knee and looked with liquid, loving eyes into his face, Max glanced round the room and saw a strange transformation. The walls widened, the ceiling rose to a greater height, and was crossed by great black beams. On the walls hung shields, spears, great swords, and numerous other articles of war and of the chase.

The polished grate had grown into an immense fireplace, and the floor was covered with what Max supposed were rushes. But the people in the room interested him most of all. On the opposite side of the fireplace, in a great carven chair, sat a lady, young and very lovely, her dress some rich dark green material clasped at the throat and waist by heavy golden clasps, her bare arms heavy with gold armlets, her long black hair falling in shining waves around her, and her eyes, the sea was in them, grey or dark blue, and in moments of anger flashing greenish yellow like the eyes of some animal.

She sat with her elbow on the arm of her chair, her head resting on her hand, looking into the fire and listening to the music of an ancient harper, who sat in the background, softly striking the chords of his harp.

The firelight, dancing over the room, caused strange shadows, and Max fancied himself one of the shadows, for his chair was filled by a boy of his own age, sitting just as he had been sitting, with the great dog's head on his knee, and notwithstanding his strange dress, Max started with a feeling almost of terror, for the boy was his double. It was like seeing himself in the glass.

A storm was raging around the castle, and above the soft music of the harp could be heard the rush of the wind, and the roar of the ocean dashing at the foot of the cliff.

The lady shivered and glanced round the room. "I wish your father were home, Patrick. How glad I shall be when peace comes again."

"I wish I were old enough to lead the clan to battle, then father could remain with you."

"What? Become a dotard? Out upon you!" Her eyes flashed at the boy, and the dog, raising his head, gave a low growl. "Why do you not have that beast speared? You know I hate him," said the lady.

"He was given to me (as you know) by the good fathers at the monastery. They told me always to cherish Bran, for he would save me from demons, as well as wolves. See the silver crosses on his collar. Nothing can harm us while Bran is here."

The lady cast a look of fear and hatred at the boy and the dog. "Don't be too sure," she said. Springing to her feet, she walked back and forth through the room. Her step was smooth and graceful, and she made no sound on the rushes as she walked.

Presently there came a lull in the storm, and from somewhere back in the hills came the howl of a wolf. The lady paused and listened, then turning to the boy she said in a hurried manner, while her eyes sought the floor: "I feel ill. I am going to my room. Let no one disturb me tomorrow. If I need help I will call." And as she turned to leave the room, suddenly she paused. "Get to bed, Patrick, and chain up that dog. You are the hope and pride of your father, and I lay my commands on you…do not hunt tomorrow."

Then the lady was gone, but Bran was trembling and growling. "He heard the wolves howl," said Patrick to the harper. The old man looked into the fire and was silent.

Presently Patrick arose, and bidding the harper good-night, went to his room, closely followed at the heels by the great dog. To his surprise, awaiting him in his room was the housekeeper, an ancient woman, who had been his father's nurse. She rose when Patrick entered, and came toward him.

"My mind is troubled, child," she said, "I must tell you my story."

"What is it, nurse?"

"It is about my lady Eileen, your stepmother. May I speak?"

"Tell on," said Patrick. "But remember, I will hear nothing against my lady," for he well knew that the nurse bore the young stepmother no good will.

"Well, listen, child. You were not here when your father married my lady. You had not left the monastery where your father placed you for safety while he was beyond seas. I must tell you first how she came here.

"Fingal, the huntsman, told me that one day, when your father was hunting alone, he was followed all day by a wolf. It would lurk from one hillock to another, but when he turned to pursue it, it would disappear. Finally, at noon, when he sat down to rest, it came creeping and fawning to his feet. He was tempted to spear it, but did not, out of surprise. Presently it disappeared, but in the gloaming it returned, and followed him clear to the gate of the castle. This my lord told to Fingal, and greatly did he marvel. That same night," whispered the nurse, mysteriously, "came a call for help, and when the gate was opened, there stood a beautiful woman (my lady Eileen) who told how she had lost her way and her company as she journeyed to St. Hilda's shrine. Your father bade her enter, and she has lived here ever since, for soon he married her, and she became our lady."

"Well, well, nurse, I knew of her coming, and I know also that she was no waif, but of a noble house and high lineage, as her coat of arms bears witness, a wolf couchant. But why explain all this to you? Right glad am I that she came to gladden my father's heart and brighten our home."

"Yes, child, but listen; this only brings me to my story. My lady has strange spells of illness, and always after a wolf howls." The boy started impatiently, but the old dame, laying her hand on his arm, compelled him to listen. "The last time it was moonlight. I was up in the turret opposite her window. Her lamp was lit, and I saw a strange sight. My lady was springing with long leaps backward and forward over the floor, and wringing her hands. Presently she went to her closet, took from it a wolf's skin, slipped it over her dress, and I do not know how she got outside the walls, but I saw her presently speeding away with long leaps toward the hills."

"Nurse, nurse, are you crazy? It is my lady of whom you speak. Never let me hear you breathe that story again. Think of my father's wrath, should this come to his ears."

Still the old woman shook her head and mumbled in wrath, and speedily took herself away, while Patrick, laughing heartily at her foolish story, went to bed. But all night above the roar of the storm could be heard the howling of wolves.

The morning broke wild and gloomy, and the castle seemed lonely and dreary without the cheery presence of Lady Eileen. Patrick went once to her door and knocked, but received no answer. Presently Fingal, the huntsman, came in, armed for the chase. Bran followed close at his heels. "Will my lord hunt today? The wolves were among the flocks last night, the shepherds tell me."

Patrick hesitated, remembering his lady's commands, but he decided finally to go. Soon he was ready, and issuing from the gates, he and Fingal and the dog were lost in the mists that enveloped the hills.

Long did the household wait their return. The night was brooding over the castle when Fingal's horn was heard at the gate. In answer to the warder's call his voice came sternly through the night, "Bring help, and come quickly, my lady is dead." To the grievous outcries and questions that arose he would return no answer.

Soon an excited group were hurrying toward the hills, and presently the torches revealed a sad sight. The first to come into view was their young lord, crouching on the ground, with the dog's head clasped in his arms; Bran's throat had been torn and mangled, and he had been thrust through with a spear. Patrick was wounded and torn in many places. Blood was flowing down his face and throat, and his tears were falling on the dog's head. Not far away lay Lady Eileen, quite dead. Very beautiful and placid she looked, as if sleeping, but on her throat were marks of great teeth.

"Take up my lady and bear her to the castle," said Patrick. "As for Bran, you must bury him here."

"Nay, child, he is only a dead dog," said the old nurse, fussily. But she was met by a stern command to be quiet.

"Do as I bid you," he said to the servants, and then added, "The good dog went mad, and attacked my lady. I could not save her. Let my father know this, should I die;" and then the boy fell backward, fainting.

To the father it was a sad home-coming when, a few days later, he returned from war. His beautiful young wife lay cold and dead in the chapel, and his son was very ill, calling always for Bran to save him from some deadly peril.

Greatly the household marvelled how their lady came to be out in the mist and the storm, alone on the hills, but Fingal, the huntsman, sought his two gossips, the nurse and the harper, and told this tale of the day's hunt.

"We had followed the wolves all day, and several had been killed. But there was one grey wolf, who seemed the leader of the pack. This one my lord singled out, and followed from valley to valley.

Bran would not pursue it, but slunk and cowered after his master, whining pitifully. All day we followed it, until, late in the gloaming, it had headed toward the castle, and we pressed it hard. It finally turned at bay, and, springing at my lord's throat, it brought him to the ground. Bran was lagging behind, and I was urging him forward. When he heard my lord's cries, the dog flew at the wolf. The beast then turned on the dog, and as I ran to help to spear it, I saw…" here the huntsman's voice sank into a whisper. "I saw no wolf, but my lady, tearing and rending the dog, while Bran's teeth were buried in her throat.

"'Separate them! Save them!' cried my lord, and I, not knowing what else to do, watched my chance and thrust the dog through the body. He sank without a groan, relaxing his grasp on my lady's throat. My lord gave a cry of despair, and my lady, hearing it, crept over to him and whispering, 'Forgive me for I could not help it,' sank dead at his feet. But Lord Patrick passed her by, and threw himself down by the dog; while I, half distraught, came home for help."

Then said the nurse, "See that you hold your tongue, man, for if this story come to the ears of my lord, your body will want a head."

But from that time forth the Lady Eileen was spoken of as "The Wolf Lady," and in time, the grim name of the "Wolf's Castle" clung to her old home.

In the years that came and passed, Patrick became chief in his father's place, and then a cairn was raised over the body of the faithful dog.

Max awoke to find the fire out. He shivered, and sprang to his feet, sating, "What a strange dream!"

Concerning Bran

An Irish Tale

This tale has been adapted from Jane Francesca Agnes Wilde's book, Ancient legends, Mystic Charms & Superstitions of Ireland, published by Chatto And Windus, London in 1919.

The Irish wolf-dog had a lithe body, a slender head, and was fleet as the wind. The form of the animal is produced constantly in Irish ornamentation, but the body always terminates in endless twisted convolutions. The great Fionn Ma-Coul had a celebrated dog called "Bran," who is thus described in the bardic legends: "A ferocious, small-headed, white-breasted, sleek-haunched hound; having the eyes of a dragon, the claws of a wolf, the vigour of a lion, and the venom of a serpent."

In the same poem Fionn himself is described in highly ornate bardic language, as he leads the hound by a chain of silver attached to a collar of gold: "A noble, handsome, fair-featured Fenian prince; young, courteous, manly, puissant; powerful in action; the tallest of the warriors; the strongest of the champions; the most beautiful of the human race."

Bran, like his master, was gifted in a remarkable degree with the foreknowledge of evil, and thus he was enabled to give his young lord many warnings to keep him from danger.

Once, when victory was not for the Fenian host, Bran showed the deepest sorrow.

"He came to Fionn, wet and weary, and by this hand," says the chronicler, "his appearance was pitiful. He lay down before the chief, and cried bitterly and howled.

"'Tis likely, my dog," says Fionn, "that our heads are in great danger this day."

Another time, the Fenian host having killed a huge boar, Ossian, the bard and prophet, ordered it to be burnt as of demon race. Bran, hearing this, went out readily and knowingly, and he brings in three trees in his paw; no one knew from where; but the trees were put into the fire and the great pig was burnt, and the ashes of the beast were cast into the sea.

The Fenian princes generally went to the hunt accompanied altogether by about three thousand hounds; Bran leading, the wisest and fleetest of all. The chiefs formed a goodly army, a thousand knights or more, each wearing a silken shirt and a *chotan* of fine silk, a green mantle and fine purple cloak over to protect it; a golden diademed helmet on the head, and a javelin in each man's hand.

Once, a chief, being jealous of the splendour of the Fenian princes, became their bitter enemy, and set himself to curse Bran above all hounds in the land.

But Fionn answered, "If you should curse Bran, my wise, intelligent dog, not a room east or west in your great mansion but I will burn with fire."

So Bran rested on the mountain with Fionn, his lord and master, and was safe from harm.

Yet, so fate decreed, Bran finally met his death by means of a woman. One day a snow-white hart, with hoofs that shone like gold, was scented on the hill, and all the hounds pursued, Bran leading.

Hour after hour passed by, and still the hart fled on, the hounds following, till one by one they all dropped off from weariness, and not one was left save Bran.

Then the hart headed for the lake, and reaching a high cliff, she plunged from it straight down into the water; the noble hound leaped in at once after her, and seized the hart as she rose to the surface; but at that instant she changed into the form of a beautiful lady, and laying her hand upon the head of Bran, she drew him down beneath the water, and the beautiful lady and Fionn's splendid hound disappeared together and were seen no more.

But in memory of the event the cliff from which he leaped is called Coegg-y-Bran; while the lake and the castle beside it are called *Tiernach Bran* (the lordship of Bran) to this day. So the name and memory of Fionn's hound, and his wisdom and achievements are not forgotten by the people; and many dogs of the chase are still called after him, for the name is thought to bring luck to the hunter and sportsman.

But the *Cailleach Biorar* (the Hag of the Water) is held in much dread, for it is believed that she still lives in a cave on the hill, and is ready to work her evil spells whenever opportunity offers, and her house is shown under the cairn, also the beaten path she traversed to the lake. Many efforts have been made to drain the lake, but the Druid priestess, the Hag of the Water, always interferes, and casts some spell to prevent the completion of the work. The water of the lake has, it is said, the singular property of turning the hair a silvery white; and the great Fionn having once bathed therein, he emerged a withered old man, and was only restored to youth by means of strong spells and incantations.

Dog Tails – Canine Fairy Tales, Myths And Legends

The Coin-Sith

A Scottish Tale

This tale is my own version of a traditional Scottish legend that probably has its roots in old Celtic and Hebridean storytelling.

In the misty glens of the Scottish Highlands, nestled among ancient forests and winding rivers, there dwelled a mystical creature known as the Coin-Sith, or Fairy Dog. It was said to be a creature of great beauty and mystery, with fur as soft as moonlight and eyes that sparkled like stars.

Legend had it that the Coin-Sith was a guardian of the faerie realm, watching over the enchanted forests and guiding lost travellers back to safety. But for those who dared to cross its path, the Coin-Sith could be both friend and foe, offering blessings to those who showed kindness and bringing misfortune to those who dared to harm it.

Among the villagers who lived near the edge of the forest was a young girl named Elsie. She had heard tales of the Coin-Sith since she was a child, but she had never encountered the creature herself. Curious and adventurous by nature, Elsie longed to catch a glimpse of the elusive faerie dog and uncover the secrets of the enchanted forest.

One moonlit night, as the mist hung low and the stars twinkled overhead, Elsie ventured into the forest alone, her heart pounding with excitement. She wandered deeper and deeper into the woods, following the faint sound of a haunting melody that seemed to float on the night air.

As she wandered deeper into the forest, Elsie stumbled upon a clearing bathed in moonlight, and there, standing before her, was the Coin-Sith. The creature was even more magnificent than she had imagined, its fur shimmering in the moonlight and its eyes filled with an otherworldly wisdom.

For a moment, Elsie stood transfixed, unable to tear her eyes away from the creature before her. But then, summoning her courage, she stepped forward and reached out to touch the faerie dog's soft fur.

To her surprise, the Coin-Sith nuzzled her hand, its touch gentle and reassuring. In that moment, Elsie felt a deep connection with the mystical creature, as if they shared a bond that transcended time and space.

From that day forth, Elsie and the Coin-Sith became unlikely companions, exploring the enchanted forest together and unravelling its many mysteries. With the faerie dog by her side, Elsie discovered hidden glens and secret pathways that she had never known existed, and she felt a sense of wonder and awe unlike anything she had ever experienced before.

But as she grew older, Elsie began to realize that her time in the enchanted forest was drawing to a close. It was time for her to return to the village and fulfil her responsibilities as a member of her community.

With a heavy heart, Elsie bid farewell to the Coin-Sith, knowing that she would never forget the magical adventures they had shared together. And though she returned to the village as a grown woman, her spirit remained forever intertwined with the enchanted forest and the mystical creature known as the Coin-Sith.

And so, the legend of the faerie dog lived on in the hearts of the villagers, a testament to the power of friendship, adventure, and the enduring magic of the Scottish Highlands.

The Dog and His Shadow

Aesop's Fable

This tale is adapted from The Talking Beasts: A Book of Fable Wisdom, which is a collection of fables compiled and edited by Kate Douglas Wiggin and her sister, Nora Archibald Smith. Published by Houghton Mifflin Company in New York and Boston in 1911, this anthology brings together a variety of traditional and lesser-known fables from around the world, featuring animals as the main characters.

A Dog, bearing in his mouth a piece of meat that he had stolen, was once crossing a smooth stream by means of a plank. Looking into the still, clear water, he saw what he took to be another dog as big as himself, carrying another piece of meat.

Snapping greedily to get this as well, he let go the meat that he already had, and it fell to the bottom of the stream.

The Three Black Dogs

An Austrian Tale

This story has been adapted from Rachel Harriette Busk's version that originally appeared in Household stories from the Land of Hofer, published in 1871 by Griffith and Farran, London.

The wind roared through the tall fir-trees, and swept the snow-flakes in masses against the window-panes. The rafters rattled and the casements clattered, but dismally, above the roaring and the clattering, sounded the howling of three black dogs at the cottage-door, for their good master lay on the pallet within, near his end, and never more should he urge them on to the joyous hunt.

The old man was stark and grey. He held the bed clothes tightly in one bony, and one rested in benediction on the dark locks of his only son kneeling by his side. Long he lay as if at the last gasp. Then suddenly raising his weary head from the pillow, he exclaimed, "Jössl, my son, do not forget to pray for your father when he is no more."

And Jössl sobbed in reply.

"Jössl," continued the old man, with painful effort, "you know fortune has never favoured me in this world. You are my noble boy, and I would have left you rich enough to be a great man, as your looks would have you, but it was not to be! Jössl, it was not to be!" and the old man sank back upon the bed, and hid his face and wept.

"Father, you have taught me to labour, to be honest, to face danger, and to fear God!" said the brave youth, throwing himself upon his father and caressing his hollow cheeks. "That was the best inheritance you could leave me."

"Well said, my noble son," replied the father. "But you are young to rough the world by yourself, and I have nothing to leave you but the Three Black Dogs, my faithful dogs, who are howling my death-knell without. Let them in, Jössl, for they are all you have now in the world!"

Jössl went to let them in, and as he did so the old man's eyes glazed over and his spirit fled, and Jössl returned to find only a corpse.

The Three Black Dogs ceased their howling when they saw his grief, and came and fawned upon him and licked his hands. For three days they remained mourning together, and then the men came and buried the father. Other people came to live in the cottage, and Jössl went out to wander over the wide world, the Three Black Dogs following behind.

When there was a day's work to be done they fared well enough. Though he had so fair a face and so noble a bearing, Jössl was always ready to apply his stalwart limbs to labour, and what he earned he shared with the Three Black Dogs, who whined and fawned and seemed to say, "We are eating your bread in idleness now, but never mind, the day will come when we earn you yours."

But when there was no work to be had, when the storm beat and the winter wind raged, Jössl was forced to share a peasant's meal where he could find pity by the way, and many there were who said, "God be gracious to you, my son," when they saw his comely face, but the Black Dogs slunk away, as if ashamed that their master's son should have to beg, not only for himself, but for them too.

Better times came with the spring, and then there was the hay-cutting, and the harvesting, and the vintage, and Jössl found plenty of work. But still he journeyed on, and the Three Black Dogs followed on behind.

At last he saw in the distance the towers of a great city, and he hasted on, for all his life he had lived in the mountains, and had never seen a town.

But when he reached it, he found that though it was a vast city, it was empty and desolate. Broad well-paved roads crossed it, but they were more deserted than the mountain-tracks. There were workshops, and smithies, and foundries, and ovens, but all were silent and empty, and no sound was heard. Then he looked up, and saw that every house was draped with black, and black banners hung from the towers and palaces.

Still not a human being appeared, either in the public squares or at the house-windows, so he still wandered on, and the Three Black Dogs followed on behind.

At last he saw in the distance a waggoner with his team coming through the principal road which traversed the city, and lost no time in making his way up to him and asking what this unearthly stillness meant.

The waggoner cracked his whip and went on, as if he were frightened and in a hurry, but Jössl kept up with him. So he told him, as they went along, that for many years past a great Dragon had devastated the country, eating up all the inhabitants he found in the way, so that everyone shunned the streets; nor should he be going through now, but that need obliged him to pass that way, and he got through the place as quickly as he could. But, he added, there was less danger for him now, because lately they had found that if every morning someone was put in his way to devour, that served him for the day, and he left off teasing and worrying others as he had been used to do, so that now a lot was cast every day, and upon whomsoever of the inhabitants the lot fell, he had to go out upon the highway early the next morning that the dragon might devour him and spare the rest.

Just then a crier came into the street, and proclaimed that the lot that day had fallen on the king's daughter, and that tomorrow morning she must be exposed to the dragon.

The people, who had come to the windows to hear what the crier had to say, now no longer kept within doors. Everyone was so shocked to think that the lot had fallen on their beautiful young princess, that they all came running out into the streets to bewail her fate aloud, and the old king himself came into their midst, tearing his clothes and plucking out his white hair, while the tears ran fast down his venerable beard.

When Jössl saw that, it reminded him of his own father, and he could not bear to see his tears.

Then the king sent the crier out again to proclaim that if anyone would fight the dragon, and deliver his daughter, he should have her hand, together with all his kingdom. But the fear of the dragon was so great on all the people of the city that there was not one who would venture to encounter it, even for the sake of such a prize.

Every hour through the day the crier went out and renewed the proclamation. But everyone was too much afraid of the dragon to make the venture, and Jössl, though he felt he would have courage to meet the dragon; could not find heart to come forward before all the people of the king's court, and profess to do what no one else could do. So the hours went by all through the day and all through the night, and no one had appeared to deliver the princess.

Then daybreak came, and with it the mournful procession which was to conduct the victim to the outskirts of the city, and all the people came out to see it, weeping. The old king came down the steps of the palace to deliver up his daughter, and it was all the people could do to hold him back from giving himself up in her place.

But when the moment of parting from her came, the thought was so dreadful that he could not bring himself to make the sacrifice, and when he should have given her up he only clasped her the tighter in his arms. Then the people began to murmur. They said, "The hour is advancing, and the dragon will be upon us, and make havoc among us all. When the lot fell upon one of us, we gave up our wives, and our fathers, and our children, and now the same misfortune has visited you, you must do no less;" and as the time wore on they grew more and more angry and discontented.

This increased the distress and terror of the king, and he raved with despair.

When Jössl found matters as bad as this, he forgot his bashfulness, and coming forward through the midst of the crowd, he asked permission to go out to meet the dragon. "And if I fail," he added, "at least I shall have prolonged the most precious life by one day;" and he bent down and kissed the hem of the princess's garment.

When the princess heard his generous words she took heart, and looked up, and was glad to see one of such noble bearing for her deliverer. But the old king, without stopping to look at him, threw himself on his neck and kissed him with delight, and called him his son, and promised him there was nothing of all the crier had proclaimed that should not be fulfilled.

The discontent of the people was changed into admiration, and they accompanied Jössl to the city gates with shouts of encouragement as he went forth to meet the dragon, and the Three Black Dogs followed on behind.

If the king's daughter had been pleased with the appearance of her deliverer, Jössl had every reason to be no less delighted with that of the lady to whom he was about to devote his life.

Full of hope and enthusiasm, he passed on through the midst of the people, regardless of their shouts, for he was thinking only of her, while the Three Black Dogs followed on behind.

It was past the time when the dragon usually received his victim, and he was advancing rapidly towards the city walls, roaring horribly, and swinging the scaly horrors of his folded tail. The fury of the monster might have made a more practised arm tremble, but Jössl thought of his father's desire that he should be a great man, and do brave deeds, and his courage only seemed to grow as the danger approached. He walked so straight towards the dragon, with a step so firm and so unlike the trembling gait of his usual victims, that it almost disconcerted the creature.

When they had approached each other within a hundred paces, Jössl called to his dog Lightning, "At him, good dog!" At the first sound of his voice Lightning sprang to the attack, and with such celerity that the dragon had no time to decide how to meet his antagonist.

"Fetch him down, Springer!" cried Jössl next, and the second dog, following close on Lightning's track, sprang upon the dragon's neck, and held him to the ground.

"Finish him, Gulper!" shouted Jössl, and the third dog, panting for the order, was even with the others in a trice, and fixing his great fangs in the dragon's flesh, snapped his spine like glass, and bounded back with delight to his master's feet.

Jössl, only stopping to caress his dogs, drew his knife, and cut out the dragon's tongue, and then returned to the city with his trophy, and the Three Black Dogs followed on behind.

If the people had uttered jubilant shouts when he started, how much more now at his victorious return! The king and his daughter heard the shout in their palace, and came down to meet the conqueror.

"Behold my daughter!" said the old king, "take her; she is yours, and my kingdom with her! I owe all to you, and in return I give you all I have."

"Nay, sire," interposed Jössl; "that you give me permission to approach the princess is all I ask, and that she will deign to let me think that I may be one day found not unworthy of her hand. But as regards your kingdom, that is not for me. I am but a poor lad, and have never had anything to command but my Three Black Dogs. How should I, then, order the affairs of a kingdom?"

The king and all the people, and the princess above all, were pleased with his modesty and grace, and they sounded his praises, and those of his Three Black Dogs too, and conducted them with him to the palace, where Jössl received a suit of embroidered clothes and the title of duke, and was seated next the princess.

The king, finding that he was resolute in refusing to accept the crown, determined to adopt him for his son, and had him instructed in everything becoming a prince, so that he might be fit to succeed him at his death. To the Three Black Dogs were assigned three kennels and three collars of gold, with three pages to wait on them, and whenever Jössl went on a hunting-party, his Three Black Dogs had precedence of all the king's dogs.

As time wore on Jössl had other opportunities of distinguishing himself, and by little and little he came to be acknowledged as the most accomplished courtier and the most valiant soldier in the kingdom.

The princess had admired his good looks and his self-devotion from the first, but when she found him so admired and courted by all the world too, her esteem and her love for him grew every day, till at last she consented to fulfil the king's wish, and they were married with great pomp and rejoicing. Never was there a handsomer pair, and never was there a braver procession of lords and ladies and attendants, than that which followed them that day, with music and with bells, and the Three Black Dogs behind.

The Dog and the Crocodile

Aesop's Fable

This tale is adapted from The Talking Beasts: A Book of Fable Wisdom, which is a collection of fables compiled and edited by Kate Douglas Wiggin and her sister, Nora Archibald Smith. Published by Houghton Mifflin Company in New York and Boston in 1911, this anthology brings together a variety of traditional and lesser-known fables from around the world, featuring animals as the main characters.

A Dog, running along the banks of the Nile, grew thirsty, but fearing to be seized by the monsters of that river, he would not stop to satiate his drought, but lapped as he ran.

A Crocodile, raising his head above the surface of the water, asked him why he was in such a hurry. He had often, he said, wished for his acquaintance, and should be glad to embrace the present opportunity.

"You do me great honour," said the Dog, "but it is to avoid such companions as you that I am in so much haste!"

Dog Tails – Canine Fairy Tales, Myths And Legends

The Dog And The Root Digger

A Blackfoot Indian Tale

This story has been edited and adapted from George Bird Grinnell's book, Blackfeet Indian Stories, first published in 1912 by Richard G. Badger at Charles Scribner's and Sons, New York.

This happened long ago. In those days the people were hungry. No buffalo could be found, and no antelope were seen on the prairie. Grass grew in the trails where the elk and the deer used to travel. There was not even a rabbit in the brush. Then the people prayed, "Oh, Napi, help us now or we must die. The buffalo and the deer are gone. It is useless to kindle the morning fires. Our arrows are useless to us. Our knives remain in their sheaths."

Then Napi set out to find where the game was, and with him went a young man, the son of a chief. For many days they travelled over the prairies. They could see no game, and roots and berries were their only food. One day they climbed to the crest of a high ridge, and as they looked off over the country they saw far away by a stream a lonely lodge.

"Who can it be?" asked the young man. "Who camps there alone, far from friends?"

"That," said Napi, "is he who has hidden all the animals from the people. He has a wife and a little son."

Then they went down near to the lodge and Napi told the young man what to do. Napi changed himself into a little dog, and he said, "This is I."

The young man changed himself into a root digger and he said, "This is I."

Pretty soon the little boy, who was playing about near the lodge, found the dog and carried it to his father, saying, "See what a pretty little dog I have found."

The father said, "That is not a dog, so throw it away!"

The little boy cried, but his father made him take the dog out of the lodge. Then the boy found the root digger, and again picking up the dog, he carried both into the lodge, saying, "Look, mother; see what a pretty root digger I have found."

"Throw them away," said his father; "throw them both away. That is not a root digger; that is not a dog."

"I want that root digger," said the woman. "Let our son have the little dog."

"Let it be so, then," replied the husband; "but remember that if trouble comes, it is you who have brought it on yourself and on our son."

Soon after this the woman and her son went off to pick berries, and when they were out of sight the man went out and killed a buffalo cow and brought the meat into the lodge and covered it up. He took the bones and the skin and threw them in the water. When his wife came back he gave her some of the meat to roast, and while they were eating, the little boy fed the dog three times, and when he offered it more the father took the meat away.

In the night, when all were sleeping, Napi and the young man arose in their right shapes and ate some of the meat.

"You were right," said the young man. "This is surely the person who has hidden the buffalo."

"Wait," said Napi, and when they had finished eating they changed themselves again into the root digger and the dog.

Next morning the wife and the little boy went out to dig roots, and the woman took the root digger with her, while the dog followed the little boy.

As they travelled along looking for roots, they passed near a cave, and at its mouth stood a buffalo cow. The dog ran into the cave, and the root digger, slipping from the woman's hand, followed, gliding along over the ground like a snake. In this cave were found all the buffalo and the other game. They began to drive them out, and soon the prairie was covered with buffalo, antelope, and deer. Never before were so many seen.

Soon the man came running up, and he said to his wife, "Who is driving out my animals?" The woman replied, "The dog and the root digger are in there now."

"Did I not tell you," said her husband, "that those were not what they looked like. See now the trouble that you have brought upon us!"

He put an arrow on his string and waited for them to come out, but they were cunning, and when the last animal, a big bull, was starting out the stick grasped him by the long hair under the neck and coiled up in it, and the dog held on by the hair underneath until they were far out on the prairie, when they changed into their true shapes and drove the buffalo toward the camp.

When the people saw the buffalo coming they led a big band of them to the piskun, but just as the leaders were about to jump over the cliff a raven came and flapped its wings in front of them and croaked, and they turned off and ran down another way. Every time a herd of buffalo was brought near to the piskun this raven frightened them away. Then Napi knew that the raven was the person who had kept the buffalo hidden.

Napi went down to the river and changed himself into a beaver and lay stretched out on a sandbar, as if dead. The raven was very hungry and flew down and began to pick at the beaver. Then Napi caught it by the legs and ran with it to the camp, and all the chiefs were called together to decide what should be done with the bird.

Some said, "Let us kill it," but Napi said, "No, I will punish it," and he tied it up over the lodge, right in the smoke hole.

As the days went by the raven grew thin and weak and its eyes were blinded by the thick smoke, and it cried continually to Napi asking him to pity it. One day Napi untied the bird and told it to take its right shape, and then said, "Why have you tried to fool Napi? Look at me. I cannot die. Look at me. Of all peoples and tribes I am the chief. I cannot die. I made the mountains; they are standing yet. I made the prairies and the rocks, and you see them yet.

"Go home now to your wife and your child, and when you are hungry hunt like anyone else. If you do not, you shall die."

The Dog in the Manger

Aesop's Fable

This tale is adapted from The Talking Beasts: A Book of Fable Wisdom, which is a collection of fables compiled and edited by Kate Douglas Wiggin and her sister, Nora Archibald Smith. Published by Houghton Mifflin Company in New York and Boston in 1911, this anthology brings together a variety of traditional and lesser-known fables from around the world, featuring animals as the main characters.

There was once a Dog who lay all day long in a manger where there was plenty of hay. It happened one day that a Horse, a Cow, a Sheep, and a Goat came one by one and wanted to eat the hay.

The Dog growled at them and would not let them have so much as a mouthful.

Then an Ox came and looked in, but the Dog growled at him also.

"You selfish fellow," said the Ox; "you cannot eat the hay. Why do you want to keep it all to yourself?"

The Golden Beetle Or Why The Dog Hates The Cat

A Chinese Tale

This story has been adapted from Norman Hinsdale Pitman's version that originally appeared in A Chinese Wonder Book, published in 1919 by E. P. Dutton And company, New York. A Chinese Wonder Book contains a selection of stories that capture the essence of traditional Chinese culture and storytelling. The book includes tales of magic, dragons, heroes, and supernatural creatures, all woven together with elements of Chinese mythology and folklore.

"What we shall eat tomorrow, I haven't the slightest idea!" said Widow Wang to her eldest son, as he started out one morning in search of work.

"Oh, the gods will provide. I'll find a few coppers somewhere," replied the boy, trying to speak cheerfully, although in his heart he also had not the slightest idea in which direction to turn.

The winter had been a hard one, excessive with extreme cold, deep snow, and violent winds. The Wang house had suffered greatly. The roof had fallen in, weighed down by heavy snow. Then a hurricane had blown a wall over, and Ming-li, the son, up all night and exposed to a bitter cold wind, had caught pneumonia. Long days of illness followed, with the spending of extra money for medicine. All their scant savings had soon melted away, and at the shop where

Ming-li had been employed his place was filled by another. When eventually he arose from his sick-bed he was too weak for hard labour and there seemed to be no work in the neighbouring villages for him to do. Night after night he came home, trying not to be discouraged, but in his heart feeling the deep pangs of sorrow that come to the good son who sees his mother suffering for want of food and clothing.

"Bless his good heart!" said the poor widow after he had gone. "No mother ever had a better boy. I hope he is right in saying the gods will provide. It has been getting so much worse these past few weeks that it seems now as if my stomach were as empty as a rich man's brain. Why, even the rats have deserted our cottage, and there's nothing left for poor Tabby, while old Blackfoot is nearly dead from starvation."

When the old woman referred to the sorrows of her pets, her remarks were answered by a pitiful mewing and woebegone barking from the corner where the two unfed creatures were curled up together trying to keep warm.

Just then there was a loud knocking at the gate. When the widow Wang called out, "Come in!" she was surprised to see an old bald-headed priest standing in the doorway. "Sorry, but we have nothing," she went on, feeling sure the visitor had come in search of food. "We have fed on scraps these two weeks, on scraps and scrapings, and now we are living on the memories of what we used to have when my son's father was living. Our cat was so fat she couldn't climb to the roof. Now look at her. You can hardly see her, she's so thin. No, I'm sorry we can't help you, friend priest, but you see how it is."

"I didn't come for alms," cried the clean-shaven one, looking at her kindly, "but only to see what I could do to help you. The gods have listened long to the prayers of your devoted son. They honour him because he has not waited till you die to do sacrifice for you. They have seen how faithfully he has served you ever since his illness, and now, when he is worn out and unable to work, they are resolved to reward him for his virtue. You likewise have been a good mother and shall receive the gift I am now bringing."

"What do you mean?" faltered Mrs. Wang, hardly believing her ears at hearing a priest speak of bestowing mercies. "Have you come here to laugh at our misfortunes?"

"By no means. Here in my hand I hold a tiny golden beetle which you will find has a magic power greater than any you ever dreamed of. I will leave this precious thing with you, a present from the god of filial conduct."

"Yes, it will sell for a good sum," murmured the other, looking closely at the trinket, "and will give us millet for several days. Thanks, good priest, for your kindness."

"But you must by no means sell this golden beetle, for it has the power to fill your stomachs as long as you live."

The widow stared in open-mouthed wonder at the priest's surprising words.

"Yes, you must not doubt me, but listen carefully to what I tell you. Whenever you wish food, you have only to place this ornament in a kettle of boiling water, saying over and over again the names of what you want to eat. In three minutes take off the lid, and there will be your dinner, smoking hot, and cooked more perfectly than any food you have ever eaten."

"May I try it now?" she asked eagerly.

"As soon as I am gone."

When the door was shut, the old woman hurriedly kindled a fire, boiled some water, and then dropped in the golden beetle, repeating these words again and again:

"Dumplings, dumplings, come to me,
I am thin as thin can be.
Dumplings, dumplings, smoking hot,
Dumplings, dumplings, fill the pot."

Would those three minutes never pass? Could the priest have told the truth? Her old head was nearly wild with excitement as clouds of steam rose from the kettle.

Off came the lid! She could wait no longer.

Wonder of wonders! There before her unbelieving eyes was a pot, full to the brim of pork dumplings, dancing up and down in the bubbling water, the best, the most delicious dumplings she had ever tasted. She ate and ate till there was no room left in her greedy stomach, and then she feasted the cat and the dog until they were ready to burst.

"Good fortune has come at last," whispered Blackfoot, the dog, to Whitehead, the cat, as they lay down to sun themselves outside. "I fear I couldn't have held out another week without running away to look for food. I don't know what's just happened, but there's no use questioning the gods."

Mrs. Wang fairly danced for joy at the thought of her son's return and of how she would feast him.

"Poor boy, how surprised he will be at our fortune, and it's all on account of his goodness to his old mother."

When Ming-li came, with a dark cloud overhanging his brow, the widow saw plainly that disappointment was written there.

"Come, come, lad!" she cried cheerily, "Clear up your face and smile, for the gods have been good to us and I shall soon show you how richly your devotion has been rewarded." So saying, she dropped the golden beetle into the boiling water and stirred up the fire.

Thinking his mother had gone stark mad for want of food, Ming-li stared solemnly at her. Anything was preferable to this misery. Should he sell his last outer garment for a few pennies and buy millet for her? Blackfoot licked his hand comfortably, as if to say, "Cheer up, master, fortune has turned in our favour." Whitehead leaped upon a bench, purring like a sawmill.

Ming-li did not have long to wait. Almost in the twinkling of an eye he heard his mother crying out, "Sit down at the table, son, and eat these dumplings while they are smoking hot."

Could he have heard correctly? Did his ears deceive him? No, there on the table was a huge platter full of the delicious pork dumplings he liked better than anything else in all the world, except, of course, his mother.

"Eat and ask no questions," counselled the Widow Wang. "When you are satisfied I will tell you everything."

Wise advice! Very soon the young man's chopsticks were twinkling like a little star in the verses. He ate long and happily, while his good mother watched him, her heart overflowing with joy at seeing him eventually able to satisfy his hunger. But still the old woman could hardly wait for him to finish, she was so anxious to tell him her wonderful secret.

"Here, son!" she cried eventually, as he began to pause between mouthfuls, "Look at my treasure!" And she held out to him the golden beetle.

"First tell me what good fairy of a rich man has been filling our hands with silver?"

"That's just what I am trying to tell you," she laughed, "for there was a fairy here this afternoon sure enough, only he was dressed like a bald priest. That golden beetle is all he gave me, but with it comes a secret worth thousands of cash to us."

The youth fingered the trinket idly, still doubting his senses, and waiting impatiently for the secret of his delicious dinner. "But, mother, what has this brass bauble to do with the dumplings, these wonderful pork dumplings, the finest I ever ate?"

"Baubles indeed! Brass! Fie, fie, my boy! You little know what you are saying. Only listen and you shall hear a tale that will open your eyes."

She then told him what had happened, and ended by setting all of the left-over dumplings upon the floor for Blackfoot and Whitehead, a thing her son had never seen her do before, for they had been miserably poor and had had to save every scrap for the next meal.

Now began a long period of perfect happiness. Mother, son, dog and cat, all enjoyed themselves to their hearts' content. All manner of new foods such as they had never tasted were called forth from the pot by the wonderful little beetle. Bird-nest soup, shark's fins, and a hundred other delicacies were theirs for the asking, and soon Ming-li regained all his strength, but, I fear, at the same time grew somewhat lazy, for it was no longer necessary for him to work. As for the two animals, they became fat and sleek and their hair grew long and glossy.

But alas! according to a Chinese proverb, pride invites sorrow. The little family became so proud of their good fortune that they began to ask friends and relatives to dinner that they might show off their good meals. One day a Mr. and Mrs. Chu came from a distant village. They were much astonished at seeing the high style in which the Wangs lived. They had expected a beggar's meal, but went away with full stomachs.

"It's the best stuff I ever ate," said Mr. Chu, as they entered their own tumble-down house.

"Yes, and I know where it came from," exclaimed his wife. "I saw Widow Wang take a little gold ornament out of the pot and hide it in a cupboard. It must be some sort of charm, for I heard her mumbling to herself about pork and dumplings just as she was stirring up the fire."

"A charm, eh? Why is it that other people have all the luck? It looks as if we were doomed forever to be poor."

"Why not borrow Mrs. Wang's charm for a few days until we can pick up a little flesh to keep our bones from clattering? It's fair enough play. Of course, we'll return it sooner or later."

"Doubtless they keep very close watch over it. When would you find them away from home now that they don't have to work anymore? As their house only contains one room, and that no bigger than ours, it would be difficult to borrow this golden trinket. It is harder, for more reasons than one, to steal from a beggar than from a king."

"Luck is surely with us," cried Mrs. Chu, clapping her hands. "They are going this very day to the Temple fair. I overheard Mrs. Wang tell her son that he must not forget he was to take her about the middle of the afternoon. I will slip back then and borrow the little charm from the box in which she hid it."

"Aren't you afraid of Blackfoot?"

"Pooh! He's so fat he can do nothing but roll. If the widow comes back suddenly, I'll tell her I came to look for my big hair-pin, that I lost it while I was at dinner."

"All right, go ahead, only of course we must remember we're borrowing the thing, not stealing it, for the Wangs have always been good friends to us, and then, too, we have just dined with them."

So skilfully did this crafty woman carry out her plans that within an hour she was back in her own house, gleefully showing the priest's charm to her husband. Not a soul had seen her enter the Wang house. The dog had made no noise, and the cat had only blinked her surprise at seeing a stranger and had gone to sleep again on the floor.

Great was the clamour and weeping when, on returning from the fair in expectation of a hot supper, the widow found her treasure missing. It was long before she could grasp the truth. She went back to the little box in the cupboard ten times before she could believe it was empty, and the room looked as if a cyclone had struck it, so long and carefully did the two unfortunates hunt for the lost beetle.

Then came days of hunger which were all the harder to bear since the recent period of good food and plenty. Oh, if they had only not got used to such dainties! How hard it was to go back to scraps and scrapings!

But if the widow and her son were sad over the loss of the good meals, the two pets were even more so. They were reduced to beggary and had to go forth daily upon the streets in search of stray bones and refuse that decent dogs and cats turned up their noses at.

One day, after this period of starvation had been going on for some time, Whitehead began suddenly to frisk about in great excitement.

"Whatever is the matter with you?" growled Blackfoot. "Are you mad from hunger, or have you caught another flea?"

"I was just thinking over our affairs, and now I know the cause of all our trouble."

"Do you indeed?" sneered Blackfoot.

"Yes, I do indeed, and you'd better think twice before you mock me, for I hold your future in my paw, as you will very soon see."

"Well, you needn't get angry about nothing. What wonderful discovery have you made? Is it that every rat has one tail?"

"First of all, are you willing to help me bring good fortune back to our family?"

"Of course I am. Don't be silly," barked the dog, wagging his tail joyfully at the thought of another good dinner. "Surely! Surely! I will do anything you like if it will bring Dame Fortune back again."

"All right. Here is the plan. There has been a thief in the house who has stolen our mistress's golden beetle. You remember all our big dinners that came from the pot? Well, every day I saw our mistress take a little golden beetle out of the black box and put it into the pot. One day she held it up before me, saying, 'Look, puss, there is the cause of all our happiness. Don't you wish it was yours?' Then she laughed and put it back into the box that stays in the cupboard."

"Is that true?" questioned Blackfoot. "Why didn't you say something about it before?"

"You remember the day Mr. and Mrs. Chu were here, and how Mrs. Chu returned in the afternoon after master and mistress had gone to the fair? I saw her, out of the tail of my eye, go to that very black box and take out the golden beetle. I thought it curious, but never dreamed she was a thief. Alas! I was wrong! She took the beetle, and if I am not mistaken, she and her husband are now enjoying the feasts that belong to us."

"Let's claw them," growled Blackfoot, gnashing his teeth.

"That would do no good," counselled the other, "for they would be sure to come out best in the end. We want the beetle back, that's the main thing. We'll leave revenge to human beings, for that is none of our business."

"What do you suggest?" said Blackfoot. "I am with you through thick and thin."

"Let's go to the Chu house and make off with the beetle."

"Alas, that I am not a cat!" moaned Blackfoot. "If we go there I couldn't get inside, for robbers always keep their gates well locked.

If I were like you I could scale the wall. It is the first time in all my life I ever envied a cat."

"We will go together," continued Whitehead. "I will ride on your back when we are fording the river, and you can protect me from strange animals. When we get to the Chu house, I will climb over the wall and manage the rest of the business myself. Only you must wait outside to help me to get home with the prize."

No sooner arranged than done. The companions set out that very night on their adventure. They crossed the river as the cat had suggested, and Blackfoot really enjoyed the swim, for, as he said, it took him back to his puppyhood, while the cat did not get a single drop of water on her face. It was midnight when they reached the Chu house.

"Just wait till I return," purred Whitehead in Blackfoot's ear.

With a mighty spring she reached the top of the mud wall, and then jumped down to the inside court. While she was resting in the shadow, trying to decide just how to go about her work, a slight rustling attracted her attention, and pop, one giant spring, one stretch-out of the claws, and she had caught a rat that had just come out of his hole for a drink and a midnight walk.

Now, Whitehead was so hungry that she would have made short work of this tempting prey if the rat had not opened its mouth and, to her amazement, begun to talk in good cat dialect.

"Pray, good puss, not so fast with your sharp teeth! Kindly be careful with your claws! Don't you know it is the custom now to put prisoners on their honour? I will promise not to run away."

"Pooh! What honour has a rat?"

"Most of us haven't much, I grant you, but my family was brought up under the roof of Confucius, and there we picked up so many crumbs of wisdom that we are exceptions to the rule. If you spare me, I will obey you for life, in fact, will be your humble slave." Then, with a quick jerk, freeing itself, "See, I am loose now, but honour holds me as if I were tied, and so I make no further attempt to get away."

"Much good it would do you," purred Whitehead, her fur crackling noisily, and her mouth-watering for a taste of rat steak. "However, I am quite willing to put you to the test. First, answer a few polite questions and I will see if you're a truthful fellow. What kind of food is your master eating now, that you should be so round and plump when I am thin and scrawny?"

"Oh, we have been in luck lately, I can tell you. Master and mistress feed on the fat of the land, and of course we hangers-on get the crumbs."

"But this is a poor tumble-down house. How can they afford such eating?"

"That is a great secret, but as I am in honour bound to tell you, here goes. My mistress has just obtained in some manner or other, a fairy's charm…"

"She stole it from our place," hissed the cat, "I will claw her eyes out if I get the chance. Why, we've been fairly starving for want of that beetle. She stole it from us just after she had been an invited guest! What do you think of that for honour, Sir Rat? Were your mistress's ancestors followers of the sage?"

"Oh, oh, oh! Why, that explains everything!" wailed the rat. "I have often wondered how they got the golden beetle, and yet of course I dared not ask any questions."

"No, certainly not! But listen, friend rat, you get that golden trinket back for me, and I will set you free at once of all obligations. Do you know where she hides it?"

"Yes, in a crevice where the wall is broken. I will bring it to you in a jiffy, but how shall we exist when our charm is gone? There will be a season of scanty food, I fear. Beggars' fare for all of us."

"Live on the memory of your good deed," purred the cat. "It is splendid, you know, to be an honest beggar. Now scoot! I trust you completely since your people lived in the home of Confucius. I will wait here for your return. Ah!" laughed Whitehead to herself, "luck seems to be coming our way again!"

Five minutes later the rat appeared, bearing the trinket in its mouth. It passed the beetle over to the cat, and then with a whisk was off for ever. Its honour was safe, but it was afraid of Whitehead. It had seen the gleam of desire in her green eyes, and the cat might have broken her word if she had not been so anxious to get back home where her mistress could command the wonderful kettle once more to bring forth food.

The two adventurers reached the river just as the sun was rising above the eastern hills.

"Be careful," cautioned Blackfoot, as the cat leaped upon his back for her ride across the stream, "be careful not to forget the treasure. In short, remember that even though you are a female, it is necessary to keep your mouth closed till we reach the other side."

"Thanks, but I don't think I need your advice," replied Whitehead, picking up the beetle and leaping on to the dog's back.

But alas, just as they were nearing the farther shore, the excited cat forgot her wisdom for a moment. A fish suddenly leaped out of the water directly under her nose. It was too great a temptation. Snap went her jaws in a vain effort to land the scaly treasure, and the golden beetle sank to the bottom of the river.

"There!" said the dog angrily, "What did I tell you? Now all our trouble has been in vain, all on account of your stupidity."

For a time there was a bitter dispute, and the companions called each other some very bad names, such as turtle and rabbit. Just as they were starting away from the river, disappointed and discouraged, a friendly frog who had by chance heard their conversation offered to fetch the treasure from the bottom of the stream. No sooner said than done, and after thanking this accommodating animal profusely, they turned homeward once more.

When they reached the cottage the door was shut, and, bark as he would, Blackfoot could not persuade his master to open it. There was the sound of loud wailing inside.

"Mistress is broken-hearted," whispered the cat, "I will go to her and make her happy."

So saying, she sprang lightly through a hole in the paper window, which, alas, was too small and too far from the ground for the faithful dog to enter.

A sad sight greeted the gaze of Whitehead. The son was lying on the bed unconscious, almost dead for want of food, while his mother, in despair, was rocking backwards and forwards wringing her wrinkled hands and crying at the top of her voice for someone to come and save them.

"Here I am, mistress," cried Whitehead, "and here is the treasure you are weeping for. I have rescued it and brought it back to you."

The widow, wild with joy at sight of the beetle, seized the cat in her scrawny arms and hugged the pet tightly to her bosom.

"Breakfast, son, breakfast! Wake up from your swoon! Fortune has come again. We are saved from starvation!"

Soon a steaming hot meal was ready, and you may well imagine how the old woman and her son, heaping praises upon Whitehead, filled the beast's platter with good things, but never a word did they say of the faithful dog, who remained outside sniffing the fragrant odours and waiting in sad wonder, for all this time the artful cat had said nothing of Blackfoot's part in the rescue of the golden beetle.

At last, when breakfast was over, slipping away from the others, Whitehead jumped out through the hole in the window.

"Oh, my dear Blackfoot," she began laughingly, "you should have been inside to see what a feast they gave me! Mistress was so delighted at my bringing back her treasure that she could not give me enough to eat, nor say enough kind things about me. Too bad, old fellow, that you are hungry. You'd better run out into the street and hunt up a bone."

Maddened by the shameful treachery of his companion, the enraged dog sprang upon the cat and in a few seconds had shaken her to death.

"So dies the one who forgets a friend and who loses honour," he cried sadly, as he stood over the body of his companion.

Rushing out into the street, he proclaimed the treachery of Whitehead to the members of his tribe, at the same time advising that all self-respecting dogs should from that time onwards make war upon the feline race.

And that is why the descendants of old Blackfoot, whether in China or in the countries of the West, have waged continual war upon the children and grandchildren of Whitehead, for a thousand generations of dogs have fought them and hated them with a great and lasting hatred.

Dog Mouths

A Latvian Tale

This tale is adapted from Latvian Fairy Tales, compiled by Victor von Andrejanoff and published by Arvi A. Karisto in 1909, which is a collection that brings together the rich folkloric traditions of Latvia. This book represents an effort to preserve and share the oral storytelling heritage of the Latvian people, capturing their myths, legends, and fairy tales in written form.

Once upon a time in a forested area there lived dog-nosed people, called the Koirakuono, and normal people close together. The former were hunters, the latter farmers. Once a young girl came from further away and was lost in the forest. The dog-nosed people took her to their home and fed her for a long time with nut kernels and sweet milk. Now and then they stuck a needle in the girl's arm, to see if this was already fat enough, and they greedily licked the blood oozing from the hole, just as a bear likes to lick up honey. Finally they thought their victim had gained enough weight. They rejoiced very much, ordered their mother to fry the girl while they went away to the forest.

A great fire had already been burning in the roasting oven for three days, but as there was no bread-shovel to hand the dog-nosed mother couldn't put the girl in the oven. Then the old woman sent the girl to the nearest human hut to get a big shovel. The girl, who didn't suspect anything bad, did as she was ordered. But the wife, from whom he asked for a shovel, guessed the true story and gave the girl, who was called Rauka, some good advice.

Later, when the mother of the dog-nosed children told the girl to sit on the shovel, she did this so unskilfully that it was quite impossible to put her in the oven. After several futile attempts, the old woman gave up and started barking and howling.

Then the girl said, "Why do you rattle like that? It is bad for your health. Show me rather how I have to position yourself correctly on the shovel, and then I'll do it just like that too."

It was clear to the old woman, so she lay on the shovel lengthwise, exclaiming, "This is how you do it, girl!"

In the blink of an eye it was the girl who pushed the old woman into the glowing furnace and locked the iron door. Then she pulled on her leather shoes and ran away.

When the dog-nosed people returned home, they immediately went to the oven and pulled out the supposed girl roast and began to eat, but it didn't taste good to them at all. Then they started to look at the remains and there they found a jewel that their mother always wore and a gold ring on her roasted finger.

Now everything became clear to them and cursing and howling, they set off in pursuit of the fugitive. The girl had run up to a wide stream, over which she could not jump. When she heard the cursing and howling of the approaching hounds she quickly climbed a tall tree which he was completely covered by moss and leaves.

The dog-nosed people of Koirakuono were at a loss as they stood on the riverbank, not knowing what they should do now. Then they suddenly saw the image of the girl they were looking for in the water. The spirit of the wind had separated the leaves from each other so that the girl's face stood out and reflected in the stream. In blind rage, the pursuers now began to lash out at water; howling and cursing all the while, getting angrier and angrier until they burst.

The girl, of course, climbed down from the tree knowing that she perfectly safe at last.

The Moddey Doo Or The Black Dog Of Peel Castle

A Manx Tale

This story has been adapted from Sophia Morrison's version that originally appeared in Manx Fairy Tales, published in 1911 by David Nutt, London.

In the days when Charles II was king in England and Charles, Earl of Derby, king in Mann, Peel Castle was always garrisoned by soldiers. The guard-room was just inside the great entrance gate of the castle and a passage used to lead from it, through one of the old churches, to the Captain of the Guard's room. At the end of the day one of the soldiers locked the castle gates and carried the keys through the dark passage to the captain. They would take it in turns.

About this time one and another began to notice, sometimes in one room, sometimes in another, a big Black Dog with rough curly hair. He did not belong to any person there, and nobody knew anything about him. But every night when the candles were lighted in the guard-room and the fire was burning bright, he would come from the dark passage and lay himself down by the hearth. He made no sound, but lay there till the break of day, and then he would get up and disappear into the passage. The soldiers were terrified of him at first, but after a time they were used to the sight of him and lost some of their fear, though they still looked on him as something more than mortal. While he was in the room the men were quiet and sober, and no bad words were spoken. When the hour came to carry the keys to the captain, two of them would always go together, for no man would face the dark passage alone.

One night, however, one foolish fellow had drunk more than was good for him, and he began to brag and boast that he was not afraid of the dog. It was not his turn to take the keys, but to show how brave he was he said that he would take them alone. He dared the dog to follow him.

'Let him come,' he shouted, laughing, 'I'll see whether he be dog or devil!'

His friends were terrified and tried to hold him back, but he snatched up the keys and went out into the passage. The Black Dog slowly got up from before the fire and followed him.

There was a dead silence in the guard-room, and no sound was heard but the dashing of the waves on the steep rocks of the Castle Islet.

After a few minutes, there came from the dark passage the most awful and unearthly screams and howls, but not a soldier dared to move to see what was going on. They looked at each other in horror. Presently they heard steps, and the rash fellow came back into the room. His face was ghastly pale and twisted with fear. He spoke not a word, then or afterwards. In three days he was dead and nobody ever knew what had happened to him that fearful night.

The Black Dog has never been seen again.

Cwn Annwn

A Welsh Tale

British Goblins: Welsh Folk-lore, Fairy Mythology, Legends and Traditions is a seminal work by Wirt Sikes, published by Sampson Low, Marston, Searle & Rivington in London in 1880. This book is a comprehensive compilation of Welsh folklore, exploring the rich tapestry of myths, legends, and traditions that have been passed down through generations in Wales.

The death portent called Cwn Annwn, or Dogs of Hell, is a pack of hounds which howl through the air with a voice frightfully disproportionate to their size, full of a wild sort of lamentation. There is a tradition that one of them once fell on a tombstone, but no one was able to secure it. A peculiarity of these creatures is that the nearer they are to a man the less loud their voice sounds, resembling then the voice of small beagles, and the farther off they are the louder is their cry. Sometimes a voice like that of a great hound is heard sounding among them, a deep hollow voice, as if it were the voice of a monstrous bloodhound.

Although terrible to hear, and although they are certain portents of death, the dogs are in themselves harmless. 'They have never been known to commit any mischief on the persons of either man or woman, goat, sheep, or cow.

Sometimes they are called Cwn y Wybr, or Dogs of the Sky, but the more sulphurous name is the favourite one. They are also sometimes called Dogs of the Fairies. Their origin in fairyland is traced to the famous mabinogi of Pwyll, Prince of Dyfed, but in that fascinating tale of enchantment their right to be called Cwn Annwn is clearly set forth, for they are there the hounds of a King of Annwn. There are several translations of this mabinogi in existence, and its popularity in South Wales is great, for the villages, vales, and streams mentioned in it are familiar to residents in Pembroke, Carmarthen, and Cardigan shires.

Pwyll, the Prince, was at Narberth, where his chief palace was, when he went one day to a wood in Glyn Cych. Here he sounded his horn and began to enter upon the chase, following his dogs and separating from his companions. And as he was listening to the cry of his pack, he could distinctly hear the cry of another pack, different from that of his own, and which was coming in an opposite direction. He could also discern an opening in the woods towards a level plain. and as his pack was entering the skirt of the opening he perceived a stag before the other pack. Then he saw that when the stag reached about the middle of the glade the pack in the rear came up and threw the stag on the ground. Upon this he fixed his attention on the colour of the pack, without looking at the stag, and of all the hounds in the world that he had ever seen he never saw any like them in colour. Their colour was a shining clear white, with red ears, and the whiteness of the dogs and the redness of their ears were equally conspicuous. They were the hounds of Arawn, a crowned king in the land of Annwn, the shadow-land of Hades.

The Cwn Annwn are sometimes held to be the hell-hounds which hunt the soul of the wicked man through the air, the instant it quits the body, which is a truly terrific idea to the vulgar mind. The Prophet Jones has several accounts of them. Thomas Phillips, of Trelech parish, heard them with the voice of the great dog sounding among them, and noticed that they followed a course that was never followed by funerals, which surprised him very much, as he had always heard that the Dogs of the Sky invariably went the same way that the corpse was to follow. Not long after a woman from an adjoining parish died at Trelech, and being carried to her own parish church to be buried, her corpse did actually pass the same way in which the spirit dogs had been heard to hunt.

Thomas Andrew, of the parish of Llanhiddel, heard them one night as he was coming home. He heard them coming towards him, though he saw them not. Their cry grew fainter as they drew near him, passed him, and louder again as they went from him. They went down the steeps towards the river Ebwy, and Thomas Andrew was known to be a a religious man, who would not have told an untruth for fear or for favour.

The Dog of Montargis

A French Tale

This tale is my own version of a traditional French myth.

Once upon a time, in the 14th century, a noble knight named Aubry de Montdidier lived in the kingdom of France. Aubry was known far and wide for his bravery and honour. However, jealousy brewed in his cousin's heart, who envied Aubry's reputation.

One fateful day, Aubry's cousin accused him of a crime he did not commit, that being the murder of a nobleman. Despite Aubry's protestations of innocence, the king ordered a trial by combat to determine the truth.

As Aubry prepared to face his accusers in the arena, his loyal companion, a majestic greyhound named Guinefort, stood faithfully by his side. Guinefort had been Aubry's companion since he was a pup, and their bond was unbreakable.

Sensing his master's distress and knowing Aubry's innocence, Guinefort leaped into action. With bravery and determination, the noble hound fought alongside Aubry, facing their adversaries head-on.

Despite being outnumbered and facing formidable opponents, Guinefort's courage knew no bounds. Together, Aubry and Guinefort fought valiantly, driving off their accusers and proving Aubry's innocence beyond a shadow of a doubt.

The people of Montargis, awed by Guinefort's loyalty and bravery, erected a grand statue in his honour. From that day forth, the tale of Aubry and Guinefort spread far and wide, celebrated as a testament to the unbreakable bond between humans and animals, and the enduring power of justice and loyalty. And so, their story lived on, cherished by generations as a timeless example of courage, friendship, and the triumph of good over evil.

Dogs Over The Water

A French Tale

This tale has been adapted from The Animal Story Book by Andrew Lang, published by Longmans, Green and Co. in London and New York in 1896, which is a collection of animal tales compiled and edited by Lang, who is well-known for his extensive work in folklore, fairy tales, and mythology.

No animal, not even the horse, has made itself so many friends as the dog. A whole library might be filled with stories about what dogs have done, and men could learn a great deal from the sufferings dogs have gone through for the masters that they love.

"Love me, love my dog," the proverb runs, but in general it would be much more to the point to say, "love my dog, love me." We do not know anything of the Austrian officer of whose death I am going to tell you, but after hearing what his dog did, we should all have been pleased to make the master's acquaintance.

In the early years of this century, when nearly every country in Europe was turned into a battlefield by Napoleon, there was a tremendous fight between the French and the Austrians at Castiglione in Lombardy, which was then under the Austrian yoke. The battle was hard fought and lasted several hours, but at length the Austrian ranks were broken and they had to retreat, after frightful losses on both sides. After the field had been won, Napoleon, as his custom was, walked round among the dead and dying, to see for himself how the day had gone. Not often had he performed this duty amidst a greater scene of blood and horror, and as he came to a spot where the dead were lying thickest, he saw to his surprise a small, long-eared spaniel standing with his feet on the breast of an Austrian officer, with his eyes fixed on the man's face, waiting to detect the slightest movement. Absorbed in his watch, the dog never heard the approach of the Emperor and his staff, but Napoleon called to one of his attendants and pointed out the spaniel.

At the sound of his voice the spaniel turned round, and looked at the Emperor, as if he knew that to him only he must appeal for help. And the prayer was not in vain, for Napoleon was seldom needlessly cruel. The officer was dead and beyond any aid, but the Emperor did what he could, and gave orders that the dog should be looked after by one of his own men, and the wounded Austrians carefully tended. Napoleon knew what it was to be loved as blindly by men as that officer was loved by his dog.

Nearly two years before this time, France was trembling in the power of a set of bloody ruffians, and in Paris especially no man felt his head to be safe from one hour to the other. Hundreds of harmless people were clapped into prison on the paltriest charges, and if they were not torn to pieces by infuriated crowds, they ended their lives on the guillotine.

Among the last of the victims before the fall of Robespierre, which finished the Reign of Terror, was a magistrate in one of the departments in the North of France whom everyone looked up to and respected. It may be thought that it would not have been easy to find a pretext for throwing into prison a man of such an open and honourable life, but when other things failed, a vague accusation of conspiracy against the Government was always possible, and accordingly the magistrate was arrested in his own house. No one was there to help him or to share his confinement. He had long sent away his children to places of safety, for some of his relations were in gaol like himself, and his friends dared not come forward. They could have done him no good, and would only have shared his fate. In those dark days every man had to suffer alone, and nobly they did it.

The magistrate had only one friend who ventured openly to show his affection, and even he might go no farther than the prison doors. That friend was his spaniel, who for twelve years had scarcely left his side, but though dogs were not yet proscribed, the spaniel's whining in support of his master availed nothing, and the gates were shut against him. At first he refused to believe that his master would never come back, and returned again and again with the hopes of meeting the magistrate on his way home. At last the dog's spirits gave way, and he went to the house of a friend of the family who knew him well, and received him kindly.

Even here, however, he had to be carefully hidden in case his protector should be charged with sheltering the dog of an accused person, and have to pay the penalty on the guillotine. The animal seemed to know what was expected of him, and never barked or growled as dogs love to do, and indeed he was too sad to take any interest in what was going on around him. The only bright spot in his day was towards evening when he was secretly let out, and he made straight for the gate of the prison. The gate was never opened, but he always hoped that this time it would be, and sat on and on till he felt that his chance was gone for that day.

All the prison officials knew him by sight, and were sorry for him, and one day the gaoler's heart was softened, and he opened the doors, and led him to his master's cell. It would be difficult to say which of the two was the happier, and when the time came for the prisoners to be locked up for the night, the man could scarcely tear away the dog, so closely did he cling to his master. However, there was no help for it, he had to be put outside, in case it should occur to someone in authority to make a visit of inspection to the prison.

Next evening the dog returned at the same hour and was again admitted, and when his time was up, he went home with a light heart, sure that by sunset next day he would be with his beloved master.

This went on for several weeks, and the dog, at any rate, would have been quite satisfied if it had gone on for ever. But one morning the magistrate was told that he was to be brought before his judges to make answer to his charge and receive his sentence. In the midst of a vast crowd, which dared not show sympathy even if it felt it, the magistrate pleaded for the last time, without a friend to give him courage except his dog, which had somehow forced himself through guards and crowd, and lay crouched between his legs, happy at this unexpected chance of seeing his master.

Sentence of death was pronounced, as was inevitable, and the hour of execution was not long delayed. In the wonderful way that animals always do know when something out of the common is passing, the spaniel was sitting outside the door when his master walked out for the last time, although it was long before the hour of his daily visit. Alone, of all the friends that he had known and loved, his dog went with him, and stood beside him on the steps of the guillotine, and sat at his feet when his head fell. Vaguely the spaniel was aware that something terrible had happened. His master, who had never failed him before, would not speak to him now. It was in vain to lick his hand: he got no pat in answer. But if his master was asleep, and his bed was underground, then he too must sleep by his side till the morning came and the world awoke again.

So two nights passed, and three. Then his friend, who had sheltered him during these long weeks, came to look for him, and, after much coaxing and caressing, persuaded him to return to his old hiding-place. With great difficulty he was induced to swallow some food, but the moment his protector's back was turned, he rushed out and fought his way to his master's grave.

This lasted for three months, and every day the dog looked sadder and thinner than the day before. At length his friend thought he would try a new plan with him, and tied him firmly up. But in the morning he found that the dog had, like Samson, broken through his bonds, and was lying on the grave, which he never left again. Food was brought to him, for he never came to seek it himself, and in time he refused even what was lying there before him. One day his friends found him trying to scratch up the earth where his master lay, and all at once his strength gave way, and with one howl he died, showing the two men who stood around of love that was stronger than death, and fidelity that lasted beyond the grave.

Dog Tails – Canine Fairy Tales, Myths And Legends

The Dog Who Was A Rajah

A Tale From Simla - India

This story has been edited and adapted from Alice Elizabeth Dracott's book, Simla Village Tales, first published in 1906 by John Murray, London.

A daughter was once born to a Brahmin and his wife, and from the day of its birth a dog came daily and laid down in the house.

This made the mother say, in jest, when the child would not cease crying, "Stop, or I shall give you to the dog."

The Brahmin added: "I'll give her to the dog when she grows up."

When the girl grew up, he said to the dog one day, in a fit of temper, "Here, take my daughter, and do as you wish with her."

The mother now regretted her jest, which had suggested this idea to her husband, and said, "Here, my child, take this handful of seeds, and, as you go, strew them along the road, so that I may know where to find you."

As the girl went along she scattered the seeds, and at last she arrived at a field in which was a small baoli, or well. Here she sat down, and told the dog she was thirsty.

"Go and drink from the well," said the dog.

As she approached the well the dog followed her, and they saw a ladder leading to the bottom of the well, so that they climbed down and came to a fine house with lovely gardens and flowers, and servants ready to receive them. These belonged to the dog, who was in reality a Rajah, and only assumed the shape of a dog when he left the well.

Sometime after this the Brahmin expressed a wish to go and visit his daughter. So his wife told him to follow the track of any freshly sprung-up little plants he might see.

He followed her directions, and found the small trees led to the well, and as he felt thirsty, he looked in and saw the ladder. so he descended by it, and found the dog had become a Rajah.

Going round the grounds with his daughter, he noticed a house made of gold. "What is this?" asked he.

"It is for you, my father."

So he went in and found everything perfect, except that in one of the walls was a great crack.

"That crack," explained the Rajah, who had joined them, "was caused when you first drank water at the well, and it will remain there until you undo the wrong you did your daughter in giving her to a dog, for you did not then know who he really was. To undo the wrong you must serve me as my cowherd for twelve years, after which time the crack in the wall will close up of its own accord."

The Brahmin then went to his wife and told her all that had happened, and they returned together to the Rajah, whose cows he tended for twelve years, after which the crack in the golden wall came together of itself, and thus the wrong was righted.

Grateful Dogs

An American Tale

This tale has been adapted from The Animal Story Book by Andrew Lang, published by Longmans, Green and Co. in London and New York in 1896, which is a collection of animal tales compiled and edited by Lang, who is well-known for his extensive work in folklore, fairy tales, and mythology.

A farmer in Nebraska possessed two dogs, a big one called Fanny, and a small one who was named Jolly. One winter day the farmer went for a walk and took with him his two pets. They came to a brook that ran through the farm, and was now frozen up.

Fanny crossed it without much ado, but Jolly, who was always afraid of water, distrusted the ice, and refused to follow. Fanny paused at the other side, and barked loudly to induce her companion to come, but Jolly pretended not to understand.

Then Fanny ran back to him, and tried to explain that it was quite safe, but in vain, for Jolly only looked after his master, and whimpered, upon which, Fanny, losing patience, seized him by the collar, and dragged him over.

For this kindness Jolly showed himself grateful some time afterwards.

Fanny, greedy creature, was fond of fresh eggs. When she heard a hen cackle she always ran to look for the nest, and one day she discovered one under the fruit-shed. But, alas, she could not get the beloved dainty because she was too large to go under the shed. Looking very pensive and thoughtful, she went away, and soon returned with Jolly, bringing him to the hole under the fruit shed.

Jolly, however, was stupid and did not understand. Fanny put her head in, and then her paws, without being able, with all her efforts, to reach the egg. The smaller dog, seeing that there was something in the hole, went in to look, but not caring for eggs, came out empty-handed.

Thereupon Fanny looked at him in such a sad and imploring way, that her master, who was watching them, could scarcely suppress his laughter.

At last Jolly seemed to understand what was wanted; he went under the shed again, brought out the egg, and put it before Fanny, who ate it with great satisfaction, and then both dogs trotted off together.

Mary, Queen Of Scots

A Scottish Tale

This tale has been adapted from The Animal Story Book by Andrew Lang, published by Longmans, Green and Co. in London and New York in 1896, which is a collection of animal tales compiled and edited by Lang, who is well-known for his extensive work in folklore, fairy tales, and mythology.

It was on February 8, 1587, that Mary Queen of Scots ended her eighteen years of weary captivity upon a scaffold at Fotheringhay. Carefully dressed in a robe of black velvet, with a long mantle of satin floating above it, and her head covered with a white crape veil, Mary ascended the platform, where the executioner was awaiting her. Some English nobles, sent by Queen Elizabeth to see that her orders were carried out, were standing by, alongside some of Queen Mary's faithful women. But besides these was one whose love for her was hardly less, that being the Queen's little dog, who had been her constant companion in the prison.

"He was sitting there the whole time," says an eye-witness, "keeping very quiet, and never stirring from her side, but as soon as the head was stricken off and placed upon the seat, he began to stir himself and cry out. Afterwards he took up a position between the body and the head, which he kept until someone came and removed him, and this had to be done by violence."

We are not told who took him away and tenderly washed off Mary's blood which was staining his coat, but we may be sure that it was one of the Queen's ladies who cherished everything that belonged to her, and in memory of her mistress would care for her little dog to the end of its days.

Dog Tails – Canine Fairy Tales, Myths And Legends

The Russet Dog

An Irish Tale

This story has been adapted from Joseph Jacob's version that originally appeared in More Celtic Fairy Tales, published in 1895 by David Nutt, London.

Oh, he's a rare clever fellow, is the Russet Dog. The Fox, I suppose you call him. Have you ever heard the way he gets rid of his fleas? He hunts about and he hunts about till he finds a lock of wool. Then he takes it in his mouth, and down he goes to the river and turns his tail to the stream, and goes in backwards. And as the water comes up to his haunches the little fleas come forward, and the more he dips into the river the more they come forward, till at last he has got nothing but his snout and the lock of wool above water; then the little fleas rush into his snout and into the lock of wool. Down he dips his nose, and as soon as he feels his nose free of them, he lets go the lock of wool, and so he is free of his fleas.

But that is nothing to the way in which he catches ducks for his dinner. He will gather some heather, and put his head in the midst of it, and then will slip downstream to the place where the ducks are swimming, for all the world like a piece of floating heather. Then he lets go, and, gobble, gobble, gobble, till not a duck is left alive.

And he is as brave as he is clever. It is said that once he found the bagpipes lying all alone, and being very hungry began to gnaw at them, but as soon as he made a hole in the bag, out came a squeal.

Was the Russet Dog afraid? Never a bit. All he said was: "Here's music with my dinner."

*

Now a Russet Dog had noticed for some days a family of wrens, off which he wished to dine. He might have been satisfied with one, but he was determined to have the whole lot, father and eighteen sons, but all so alike that he could not tell one from the other, or the father from the children.

"It is no use to kill one son," he said to himself, "because the old cock will take warning and fly away with the seventeen others. I wish I knew which one of them is the old gentleman."

He set his wits to work to find out, and one day seeing them all threshing in a barn, he sat down to watch them, but still he could not be sure.

"Now I have it," he said, "well done the old man's stroke! He hits true," he cried.

"Oh!" replied the one he suspected of being the head of the family, "Ff you had seen my grandfather's strokes, you might have said that."

The sly fox pounced on the cock, ate him up in a trice, and then soon caught and disposed of the eighteen sons, all flying in terror about the barn.

*

For a long time a Tod-hunter had been very anxious to catch our friend the fox, and had stopped up all the earths in cold weather. One evening he fell asleep in his hut, and when he opened his eyes he saw the fox sitting very demurely at the side of the fire. It had entered by the hole under the door provided for the convenience of the dog, the cat, the pig, and the hen.

"Oh! ho!" said the Tod-hunter, "Now I have you." And he went and sat down at the hole to prevent Reynard's escape.

"Oh! ho!" said the fox, "I will soon make that stupid fellow get up." So he found the man's shoes, and putting them into the fire, wondered if that would make the enemy move.

"I shan't get up for that, my fine gentleman," cried the Tod-hunter.

Stockings followed the shoes, coat and trousers shared the same fate, but still the man sat over the hole. At last the fox having set the bed and bedding on fire, put a light to the straw on which his jailer lay, and it blazed up to the ceiling.

"No! That I cannot stand," shouted the man, jumping up, and the fox, taking advantage of the smoke and confusion, made good his exit.

*

But Master Rory did not always have it his own way. One day he met a cock, and they began talking.

"How many tricks can you do?" said the fox.

"Well," said the cock, "I could do three. How many can you do yourself?"

"I could do three score and thirteen," said the fox.

"What tricks can you do?" said the cock.

"Well," said the fox, "my grandfather used to shut one eye and give a great shout."

"I could do that myself," said the cock.

"Do it," said the fox. And the cock shut one eye and crowed as loud as ever he could, but he shut the eye that was next the fox, and the fox gripped him by the neck and ran away with him. But the wife to whom the cock belonged saw him and cried out, "Let go the cock; he's mine."

"Say, 'Oh sweet-tongued singer, it is my own cock,' will you not?" said the cock to the fox.

Then the fox opened his mouth to say as the cock did, and he dropped the cock, who sprung up on the top of a house, and shut one eye and gave a loud crow.

*

But it was through that very fox that Master Wolf lost his tail. Have you never heard about that?

One day the wolf and the fox were out together, and they stole a dish of crowdie. Now in those days the wolf was the biggest beast of the two, and he had a long tail like a greyhound and great teeth.

The fox was afraid of him, and did not dare to say a word when the wolf ate most of the crowdie, and left only a little at the bottom of the dish for him, but he determined to punish him for it, so the next night when they were out together the fox pointed to the image of the moon in a pool left in the ice, and said, "I smell a very nice cheese, and there it is, too."

"And how will you get it?" said the wolf.

"Well, you stop you here till I see if the farmer is asleep, and if you keep your tail on it, nobody will see you or know that it is there. Keep it steady. I may be some time coming back."

So the wolf lay down and laid his tail on the moonshine in the ice, and kept it for an hour till it was stuck fast. Then the fox, who had been watching, ran into the farmer and said, "The wolf is there. He will eat up the children, the wolf, the wolf!"

Then the farmer and his wife came out with sticks to kill the wolf, but the wolf ran off leaving his tail behind him, and that's why the wolf is stumpy-tailed to this day, though the fox has a long brush.

*

One day shortly after this Master Rory chanced to see a fine cock and fat hen, off which he wished to dine, but at his approach they both jumped up into a tree. He did not lose heart, but soon began to make talk with them, inviting them at last to go a little way with him.

"There was no danger," he said, "nor fear of his hurting them, for there was peace between men and beasts, and among all animals."

At last after much parleying the cock said to the hen, "My dear, do you not see a couple of hounds coming across the field?"

"Yes," said the hen, "and they will soon be here."

"If that is the case, it is time I should be off," said the sly fox, "for I am afraid these stupid hounds may not have heard of the peace."

And with that he took to his heels and never drew breath till he reached his den.

*

Now Master Rory had not finished with his friend the wolf. So he went round to see him when his stump got better.

"It is lucky you are," he said to the wolf. "How much better you will be able to run now you haven't got all that to carry behind you."

"Away from me, traitor!" said the wolf.

But Master Rory said, "Is it a traitor I am, when all I have come to see you for is to tell you about a keg of butter I have found?"

After much grumbling the wolf agreed to go with Master Rory.

So the Russet Dog and the wild dog, the fox and the wolf, were going together, and they went round about the sea-shore, and they found the keg of butter, and they buried it.

On the morrow the fox went out, and when he returned in he said that a man had come to ask him to a baptism. He arrayed himself in excellent attire, and he went away, and where should he go but to the butter keg, and when he came home the wolf asked him what the child's name was, and he said it was HEAD OFF.

On the morrow he said that a man had sent to ask him to a baptism, and he reached the keg and he took out about half. The wolf asked when he came home what the child's name was.

"Well," said he, "it is a queer name that I myself would not give to my child, if I had him. It is HALF AND HALF."

On the morrow he said that there was a man there came to ask him to a baptism again. Off he went and he reached the keg, and he ate it all up. When he came home the wolf asked him what the child's name was, and he said it was ALL GONE.

On the morrow he said to the wolf that they ought to bring the keg home. They went, and when they reached the keg there was not a shadow of the butter in it.

"Well, surely you were coming here to watch this, when I was away?," asked the fox.

The other one swore that he had not come near it.

"You need not be swearing that you did not come here; I know that you did come, and that it was you that took it out, but I will know if it was you that ate the butter when you go home," said the fox.

Off they went, and when they got home he hung the wolf by his hind legs, with his head dangling below him, and he had a dab of the butter and he put it under the wolf's mouth, as if it was out of the wolf's belly that it came.

"You red thief!" said he, "I said before that it was you that ate the butter."

*

They slept that night, and on the morrow when they rose the fox said, "Well, then, it is silly for ourselves to be starving to death in this way merely for laziness. We will go to a town-land, and we will take a piece of land in it."

They reached the town-land, and the man to whom it belonged gave them a piece of land the worth of seven Saxon pounds.

It was oats that they set that year, and they reaped it and they began to divide it.

"Well, then," said the fox, "would you rather have the root or the tip? you shall have your choice."

"I'd rather the root," said the wolf.

Then the fox had fine oaten bread all the year, and the other one had fodder.

On the next year they set a crop, and it was potatoes that they set, and they grew well.

"Which would you like best, the root or the crop this year?" said the fox.

"Indeed, you shall not take the twist out of me anymore; I will have the top this year," said the wolf.

"Good enough, my hero," said the fox.

Thus the wolf had the potato tops, and the fox the potatoes. But the wolf used to keep stealing the potatoes from the fox.

"You had best go yonder, and read the name that I have in the hoofs of the grey mare," said the fox.

Away went the wolf, and he began to read the name, and on a time of these times the white mare drew up her leg, and she broke the wolf's head.

"Oh!" said the fox, "it is long since I heard my name, but it's better to catch geese than to read books."

He went home, and the wolf was not troubling him anymore.

*

But the Russet Dog found his match at last, as I shall tell you.

One day the fox was going over a loch, and there he met a little bonnach, and the fox asked him where he was going. The little bonnach told him he was going to such a place.

"And where have you come from?" said the fox.

"I came from Geeogan, and I came from Cooaigean, and I came from the slab of the bonnach stone, and I came from the eye of the quern, and I will come from you if I may," said the little bonnach.

"Well, I myself will take you over on my back," said the fox.

"You'll eat me, you'll eat me," said the little bonnach.

"Come then on the tip of my tail," said the fox.

"Oh no! I will not; you will eat me," said the little bonnach.

"Come into my ear," said the fox.

"I will not go, you will eat me," said the little bonnach.

"Come into my mouth," said the fox.

"You will eat me that way at all events," said the little bonnach.

"Oh no, I will not eat you," said the fox. "When I am swimming I cannot eat anything at all."

The bonnach went into the fox's mouth.

"Oh! ho!" said the fox, "I may do my own pleasure on you now. It was long ago said that a hard morsel is no good in the mouth."

The fox ate the little bonnach. Then he went to a loch, and he caught hold of a duck that was in it, and he ate that.

He went up to a hillside, and he began to stroke his sides on the hill, saying, "Oh, king! how finely a bullet would spank upon my rib just now."

Who was listening but a hunter. "I'll try that upon you directly," said the hunter.

"Bad luck to this place," said the fox, "in which a creature dares not say a word in fun that is not taken in earnest."

The hunter put a bullet in his gun, and he fired at him and killed him, and that was the end of the Russet Dog.

The Farmer and His Dog

This tale is adapted from The Talking Beasts: A Book of Fable Wisdom, which is a collection of fables compiled and edited by Kate Douglas Wiggin and her sister, Nora Archibald Smith. Published by Houghton Mifflin Company in New York and Boston in 1911, this anthology brings together a variety of traditional and lesser-known fables from around the world, featuring animals as the main characters.

A Farmer who had just stepped into the field to close a gap in one of his fences found on his return the cradle, where he had left his only child asleep, turned upside down, the clothes all torn and bloody, and his Dog lying near it smeared with blood. Convinced at once that the creature had destroyed his child, he instantly dashed out its brains with the hatchet in his hand.

When he turned up the cradle, he found the child unhurt and an enormous serpent lying dead on the floor, killed by the faithful Dog, whose courage and fidelity in preserving the life of his son deserved another kind of reward.

These affecting circumstances afforded him a striking lesson upon how dangerous it is to give way to the impulse of a sudden passion.

Why Dog And Cat Are Enemies

A Chinese Tale

This story has been adapted from Dr. Richard Wilhelm's version that originally appeared in The Chinese Fairy Book, published in 1921 by Frederick A. Stokes Company, New York. Wilhelm's translations aimed to capture the essence of the original Chinese texts while making them accessible to English-speaking audiences. His deep understanding of Chinese language and culture shone through in his translations, allowing readers to appreciate the beauty and depth of these timeless tales.

Once upon a time there was a man and his wife and they had a ring of gold. It was a lucky ring, and whoever owned it always had enough to live on. But this they did not know, and hence sold the ring for a small sum. But no sooner was the ring gone than they began to grow poorer and poorer, and at last did not know when they would get their next meal. They had a dog and a cat, and these had to go hungry as well. Then the two animals took counsel together as to how they might restore to their owners their former good fortune. At length the dog hit upon an idea.

"They must have the ring back again," he said to the cat.

The cat answered: "The ring has been carefully locked up in the chest, where no one can get at it."

"You must catch a mouse," said the dog, "and the mouse must gnaw a hole in the chest and fetch out the ring. And if she does not want to, say that you will bite her to death, and you will see that she will do it."

This advice pleased the cat, and she caught a mouse. Then she wanted to go to the house in which stood the chest, and the dog came after. They came to a broad river. And since the cat could not swim, the dog took her on his back and swam across with her. Then the cat carried the mouse to the house in which the chest stood. The mouse gnawed a hole in the chest, and fetched out the ring. The cat put the ring in her mouth and went back to the river, where the dog was waiting for her, and swam across with her. Then they started out together for home, in order to bring the lucky ring to their master and mistress. But the dog could only run along the ground. When there was a house in the way he always had to go around it. The cat, however, quickly climbed over the roof, and so she reached home long before the dog, and brought the ring to her master.

Then her master said to his wife: "What a good creature the cat is! We will always give her enough to eat and care for her as though she were our own child!"

But when the dog came home they beat him and scolded him, because he had not helped to bring home the ring again. And the cat sat by the fireplace, purred and said never a word. Then the dog grew angry at the cat, because she had robbed him of his reward, and when he saw her he chased her and tried to seize her.

And ever since that day cat and dog are enemies.

Still Waters Run Deep; Or The Dancing Dog

A French Tale

This tale has been adapted from The Animal Story Book by Andrew Lang, published by Longmans, Green and Co. in London and New York in 1896, which is a collection of animal tales compiled and edited by Lang, who is well-known for his extensive work in folklore, fairy tales, and mythology.

When Little Théophile became Big Théophile, he was as fond as ever of dogs and cats, and he knew more about them than anybody else. After the death of a large white spaniel called Luther, he filled the vacant place on his rug by another of the same breed, to whom he gave the name of Zamore. Zamore was a little dog, as black as ink, except for two yellow patches over his eyes, and a stray patch on his chest. He was not in the least handsome, and no stranger would ever have given him a second thought. But when you came to know him, you found Zamore was not a common dog at all. He despised all women, and absolutely refused to obey them or to follow them, and neither Théophile's mother nor his sisters could get the smallest sign of friendship from him. If they offered him cakes or sugar, he would accept them in a dignified manner, but never dreamed of saying 'thank you,' still less of wagging his tail on the floor, or giving little yaps of delight and gratitude, as well-brought-up dogs should do. Even to Théophile's father, whom he liked better than anyone else, he was cold and respectful, though he followed him everywhere, and never left his master's heels when they took a walk. And when they were fishing together, Zamore would sit silent on the bank for hours together, and only allowed himself one bark when the fish was safely hooked.

Now no one could possibly have guessed that a dog of such very quiet and reserved manners was at heart as gay and cheerful as the silliest kitten that ever was born, but so he was, and this was how his family found it out.

One day he was walking as seriously as usual through a broad square in the outskirts of Paris, when he was surprised at meeting a large grey donkey, with two panniers on its back, and in the panniers a troop of dogs, some dressed as Swiss shepherdesses, some as Turks, some in full court costume. The owner of the animals stopped the donkey close to where Zamore was standing, and bade the dogs jump down. Then he cracked his whip, the fife and drum struck up a merry tune, the dogs steadied themselves on their hind legs, and the dance began.

Zamore looked on as if he had been turned into stone. The sight of these dogs, dressed in bright colours, this one with his head covered by a feathered hat, and that one by a turban, but all moving about in time to the music, and making pirouettes and little bows; were they really *dogs* that he was watching or some new kind of men? Anyway he had never seen anything so enchanting or so beautiful, and if it was true that they were only dogs, well, *he* was a dog too!

With that thought, all that had lain hidden in Zamore's soul burst forth, and when the dancers filed gracefully before him, he raised himself on his hind legs, and in spite of staggering a little, prepared to join the ring, to the great amusement of the spectators.

The dog-owner, however, whose name was Monsieur Corri, did not see matters in the same light. He raised his whip a second time, and brought it down with a crack on the sides of Zamore, who ran out of the ring, and with his tail between his legs and an air of deep thought, he returned home.

All that day Zamore was more serious and gloomier than ever. Nothing would tempt him out, hardly even his favourite dinner, and it was quite plain that he was turning over something in his mind. But during the night his two young mistresses were awakened by a strange noise that seemed to come from an empty room next theirs, where Zamore usually slept. They both lay awake and listened, and thought it was like a measured stamping, and that the mice might be giving a ball. But could little mice feet tread so heavily as that? Supposing a thief had got in? So the bravest of the two girls got up, and stealing to the door softly opened it and looked into the room. And what do you think she saw? Why, Zamore, on his hind legs, his paws in the air, practising carefully the steps that he had been watching that morning!

This was not, as one might have expected, a mere fancy of the moment, which would be quite forgotten the next day. Zamore was too serious a dog for that, and by dint of hard study he became in time a beautiful dancer. As often as the fife and drum were heard in the streets, Zamore rushed out of the house, glided softly between the spectators, and watched with absorbed attention the dancing dogs who were doing their steps: but remembering the blow he had had from the whip, he took care not to join them. He noted their positions, the figures, and the way they held their bodies, and in the night he copied them, though by day he was just as solemn as ever. Soon he was not contented with merely copying what he saw, so he invented for himself, and it is only just to say that, in stateliness of step, few dogs could come up to him. Often his dances were witnessed (unknown to himself) by Théophile and his sisters, who watched him through the crack of the door, and so earnest was he, that at length, worn out by dancing, he would drink up the whole of a large basin of water, which stood in the corner of the room.

When Zamore felt himself the equal of the best of the dancing dogs, he began to wish that like them he might have an audience.

Now in France the houses are not always built in a row as they are in England, but sometimes have a square court-yard in front, and in the house where Zamore lived, this court was shut in on one side by an iron railing, which was wide enough to let dogs of a slim figure squeeze through.

One fine morning there met in this court-yard fifteen or twenty dogs, friends of Zamore, to whom the night before he had sent letters of invitation. The object of the party was to see Zamore make his début in dancing, and the ball-room was to be the court-yard, which Zamore had carefully swept with his tail. The dance began, and the spectators were so delighted, that they could not wait for the end to applaud, as people ought always to do, but uttered loud cries of 'Ouah, ouah,' that reminded you of the noises you hear at a theatre. Except one old water spaniel was filled with envy at Zamore's talents, and declared that no decent dog would ever make an exhibition of himself like that. However, they all vowed that Zamore was the king of dancers, and that nothing had ever been seen to equal his minuet, jig, and waltz for grace and beauty.

It was only during his dancing moments that Zamore unbent. At all other times he was as gloomy as ever, and never cared to stir from the rug unless he saw his old master take up his hat and stick for a walk. Of course, if he had chosen, he might have joined Monsieur Corri's _troupe, of which he would have made the brightest ornament, but the love of his master proved greater than his love of his art, and he remained unknown, except of his family. In the end he fell a victim to his passion for dancing, and he died of brain fever, which is supposed to have been caused by the fatigue of learning the schottische, the fashionable dance of the day.

The Story Of The Dog And The Snake And The Cure Of Headache

A Romanian Tale

This story has been adapted from an anonymous original translated by Moses Gaster that appeared in Rumanian Bird and Beast Stories, published in 1915 by Sidgwick & Jackson, Ltd., London.

Once upon a time, I do not know how it came about, the dog had a frightful headache, such a headache as he had never had before. It nearly drove him mad, and he ran furiously here and there, not knowing what to do to get rid of it. As he was running wildly over a field, he met a snake that was lying there coiled up in the sun.

"Why are you running about like a madman, brother?" asked the snake.

"Sister, I cannot stop to speak to you. I am clean mad with a splitting headache, and I do not know how to be rid of it."

"I know a remedy," said the snake, "it is excellent for the headache of a dog, but it is of no good to me who am also suffering greatly from a headache."

"Never mind you, what am I to do?"

"You go yonder and eat some of the grass, and you will be cured of the headache."

The dog did as the snake had advised him. He went and ate the grass, and soon felt relieved of his pain.

Now, do you think the dog was grateful? No such luck for the snake. On the contrary, a dog is a dog, and a dog he remains. And why should he be better than many people are? He did as they do, and returned evil for good. Going to the snake, he said, "Now that my headache is gone, I feel much easier. I remember an excellent remedy for the headache of snakes."

"And what might it be?" asked the snake eagerly.

"It is quite simple. When you feel your head aching, go and stretch full length across the high-road and lie still for a while, and the pain is sure to leave you."

"Thank you," said the simpleton of a snake, and she did as the dog had advised her. She stretched herself full length across the high-road and lay still, waiting for the headache to go.

The snake had been lying there for some time, when it so happened that a man came along with a stout cudgel in his hands. To see the snake and to bruise her head was the work of an instant. And the snake no longer had any headache. The cure proved complete. And ever since that time, when a snake has a headache it goes and stretches across the high-road. If its head is crushed, then no other remedy is wanted, but if the snake escapes unhurt, it loses its headache.

Story of the Buddhist monk who was bitten by a dog.

An Indian Tale

This tale is adapted from The Kathá Sarit Ságara, translated as The Ocean of the Streams of Stories, which is an 11th-century Sanskrit text by Somadeva Bhatta. It is a monumental collection of Indian legends, fairy tales, and folk tales compiled in a frame-story format. The 1884 edition published by the Baptist Mission Press is a significant English translation of this work, making it accessible to a broader audience.

There was in a certain Buddhist monastery a Buddhist monk of dull intellect. One day, as he was walking in the high road, he was bitten by a dog on the knee.

And when he had been thus bitten, he returned to his monastery, and thus reflected, "Everybody, one after another, will ask me, 'What has happened to your knee?' And what a time it will take me to inform them all one by one. So I will make use of an artifice to let them all know at once."

Having thus reflected, he quickly went to the top of the monastery, and taking the stick with which the gong was struck, he sounded the gong. And the mendicant monks, hearing it, came together in astonishment, and said to him, "Why do you without cause sound the gong at the wrong time and without cause?"

He answered the mendicants, at the same time showing them his knee, "The fact is, a dog has bitten my knee, so I called you together, thinking that it would take a long time for me to tell each of you separately such a long story, so hear it all of you now, and look at my knee."

Then all the mendicants laughed till their sides ached, and said, "What a great fuss he has made about a very small matter!"

Anubis, The Dog Headed God

An Ancient Egyptian Tale

This tale is my own version of a traditional Egyptian tale rooted in the stories told in The Book Of The Dead..

Once upon a time, in the ancient land of Egypt, there lived a god named Anubis. Anubis was a mighty and noble deity, with the head of a jackal and the body of a man. He was known as the guardian of the dead, the protector of graves, and the guide to the afterlife.

Anubis was deeply respected by the people of Egypt, who believed in his power to safeguard the souls of the departed as they journeyed to the realm of the dead. He was often depicted with a jackal's head, wearing regal robes and holding the symbols of his authority.

In the kingdom of Egypt, there was a great pharaoh named Khufu who ruled with wisdom and strength. When Pharaoh Khufu passed away, his soul embarked on a perilous journey to the afterlife. But Anubis was there to guide him, leading him through the treacherous paths of the underworld and protecting him from harm.

Anubis was also responsible for the sacred ritual of mummification, which ensured that the bodies of the deceased were preserved for their journey to the afterlife. With great care and reverence, he oversaw the embalming process, ensuring that the souls of the departed could rest peacefully in the afterlife.

Despite his solemn duties, Anubis was a kind and compassionate deity, always willing to help those in need. He watched over the people of Egypt with a watchful eye, offering guidance and protection to all who sought his aid.

And so, the legend of Anubis lived on in the hearts of the Egyptian people, who revered him as a symbol of hope and eternal life. For as long as there were souls to guide and graves to protect, Anubis would remain steadfast in his divine duty, ensuring that the spirits of the departed found peace in the afterlife.

The Black Dog And The Thumbless Hand

A Pacific Isles Tale (New Hebrides)

This tale is adapted from Andrew Lang's book, The Book of Dreams and Ghosts, published by Longmans, Green and Co. in London and New York in 1899. The book is a fascinating exploration of supernatural phenomena, particularly focusing on dreams and ghostly encounters. Lang, a prolific author and folklorist, compiled a wide range of stories and accounts that delve into the mysterious and the otherworldly.

This is a true conversation between me and my friend...

"Have the natives the custom of walking through fire?" said my friend the Beach-comber, in answer to a question of mine.

"Not that I know of. In fact the soles of their feet are so thick-skinned that they would think nothing of it."

"Then have they any spiritualistic games, like the Burmans and Maories? I have a lot of yarns about them."

"They are too jolly well frightened of bush spirits to invite them to tea," said the Beach-comber. "I knew a fellow who got a bit of land merely by whistling up and down in it at nightfall. They think spirits whistle. No, I don't fancy they go in for seances. But we once had some, we white men, in one of the islands.. And that led to Bolter's row with me."

"What about?"

"Oh, about his young woman. I told her the story. It was thoughtless, and yet I don't know that I was wrong. After all, Bolter could not have been a comfortable fellow to marry."

"Bad moral character?"

"Not that I know of. Queer fish. Kept queer company. Even if she was ever so fond of dogs, I don't think a girl would have cared for Bolter's kennel. Not in her bedroom anyway."

"But she could surely have got him to keep them outside, however doggy he was?"

"He was not doggy a bit. I don't know that Bolter ever saw the black dogs himself. He certainly never told me so. It is that beastly Thumbless Hand, no woman could have stood it, not to mention the chance of catching cold when it pulled the blankets off."

"What on earth are you talking about? I can understand a man attended by black dogs that nobody sees but himself. The Catholics tell it of John Knox, and of another Reformer, a fellow called Smeaton. Moreover, it is common in delirium tremens. But you say Bolter didn't see the dogs?"

"No, not so far as he told me, but I did, and other fellows, when with Bolter. Bolter was asleep. He didn't see anything. Also the Hand, which was a good deal worse. I don't know if he ever saw it. But he was jolly nervous, and he had heard of it."

"Tell me about it all, old cock," I said.

"I'm sure I told you last time I was at home."

"Never. My memory for yarns is only too good. I hate a chestnut."

"Well, here goes! Mind you I don't profess to explain the thing. Only I don't think I did wrong in telling the young woman, for, however one accounts for it, it was not nice."

"A good many years ago a clerk came to the island by the name of Bolter. The most curious thing about his appearance was his eyes: they were large, black, and had a peculiar dull dead lustre."

"Did they shine in the dark? I knew a fellow at Oxford whose eyes did. Chairs ran after him."

"I never noticed. I don't remember. 'Psychically,' as you superstitious muffs call it, Bolter was still more queer. At that time we were all gone on spirit-rapping. Bolter turned out a great acquisition, 'medium,' or what not. Mind you, I'm not saying Bolter was straight. In the dark he'd tell you what you had in your hand, exact time of your watch, and so on. I didn't take stock in this, and one night brought some photographs with me, and asked for a description of them. This he gave correctly, winding up by saying, 'The one nearest your body is that of ...'"

Here my friend named a person well known to both of us, whose name I prefer not to introduce here. This person, I may add, had never been in or near the island, and was totally unknown to Bolter.

"Of course," my friend went on, "the photographs were all the time inside my pocket. Now, really, Bolter had some mystic power of seeing in the dark."

"Hyperaesthesia!" said I.

"Hypercriticism!" said the Beach-comber.

"What happened next might be hyperaesthesia, by which I suppose you mean abnormal intensity of the senses, but how could hyperaesthesia see through a tweed coat and lining?"

"Well, what happened next?"

"Bolter's firm used to get sheep by every mail, and send them regularly to their station, six miles off. One time they landed late in the afternoon, and yet were foolishly sent off, Bolter in charge. I said at the time he would lose half the lot, as it would be dark long before he could reach the station, but he didn't lose any of them!

"Next day I met one of the chaps who was sent to lend him a hand, and asked results.

"'Master,' said the man, 'Bolter is a devil! He sees at night. When the sheep ran away to right or left in the dark, he told us where to follow.'"

"He heard them, I suppose," said I.

"Maybe, but you must be sharp to have sharper senses than these native chaps. Anyhow, that was not Bolter's account of it. When I saw him and spoke to him he said simply, 'Yes, that when excited or interested to seek or find anything in obscurity the object became covered with a dim glow of light, which rendered it visible'. 'But things in a pocket.' 'That also,' said he. 'Curious isn't it? Probably the Rontgen rays are implicated therein, eh?'"

"Did you ever read Dr. Gregory's Letters on Animal Magnetism?"

"The cove that invented Gregory's Mixture?"

"Yes."

"Beast he must have been. No, I never read him."

"He says that Major Buckley's hypnotised subjects saw hidden objects in a blue light, mottoes inside a nut, for example."

"Rontgen rays, for a fiver! But Bolter said nothing about seeing blue light. Well, after three or four seances Bolter used to be very nervous and unwilling to sleep alone, so I once went with him to his one-roomed hut. We turned into the same bed. I was awakened later by a noise and movement in the room. Found the door open; the full moon streaming in, making light like day, and the place full of great big black dogs. well, anyhow there were four or five!

They were romping about, seemingly playing. One jumped on the bed, another rubbed his muzzle on mine! (the bed was low, and I slept outside). Now I never had anything but love for dogs of any kind, and as love casts out fear, I simply got up, turned them all out, shut the door, and turned in again myself. Of course my idea was that they were flesh and blood, and I allude to physical fear.

"I slept, but was awakened again by a ghastly feeling that the blanket was being dragged and creeping off the bed. I pulled it up again, but the slow movement of descent began again.

"Rather surprised, I pulled it up afresh and held it, and must have dozed off, as I suppose. I awoke, to feel it being pulled again. It was slipping, slipping, and then with a sudden, violent jerk it was thrown on the floor. During all this I had glanced several times at Bolter, who seemed profoundly asleep. But now alarmed I tried to wake him. In vain, he slept like the dead. His face, always a pasty white, now like marble in the moonlight. After some hesitation I put the blanket back on the bed and held it fast. The pulling at once began and increased in strength, and I, by this time thoroughly alarmed, put all my strength against it, and hung on like grim death.

"To get a better hold I had taken a corner and pulled it over my head, when suddenly I felt a pressure outside on my body, and a movement like fingers. They gradually approached my head. Mad with fear I chucked off the blanket, grasped a Hand, gazed on it for one moment in silent horror, and threw it away! No wonder, it was attached to no arm or body, it was hairy and dark coloured, the fingers were short, blunt, with long, claw-like nails, and it was minus a thumb! Too frightened to get up I had to stop in bed, and, I suppose, fell to sleep again, after fresh vain attempts to awaken Bolter. Next morning I told him about it. He said several men who had thus passed the night with him had seen this hand. 'But,' added he, 'it's lucky you didn't have the big black dogs also!'

"I was to have slept again with him next night to look further into the matter, but a friend of his came that day, so I could not renew the experiment, as I had fully determined to do. By-the-bye, I was troubled for months after by the same feeling that the clothes were being pulled off the bed.

"And that's the yarn of the Black Dogs and the Thumbless Hand."

"I think," said I, "that you did no harm in telling Bolter's young woman."

"I never thought of it when I told her, or of her interest in the kennel, but, by George, she soon broke off her engagement."

"Did you know Manning, the Pakeha Māori, the fellow who wrote Old New Zealand?"

"No, what about him?"

"He did not put it in his book, but he told the same yarn, without the dogs, as having happened to himself. He saw the whole arm, and the hand was leprous."

"Ugh!" said the Beach-comber.

"Next morning he was obliged to view the body of an old Māori, who had been murdered in his garden the night before. That old man's hand was the hand he saw. I know a room in an old house in England where plucking off the bed-clothes goes on, every now and then, and has gone on as long as the present occupants have been there. But I only heard lately, and they only heard from me, that the same thing used to occur, in the same room and no other, in the last generation, when another family lived there."

"Anybody see anything?"

"No, only footsteps are heard creeping up, before the twitches come off."

"And what do the people do?"

"Nothing! We set a camera once to photograph the spook. He did not sit."

"It's rum!" said the Beach-comber. "But mind you, as to spooks, I don't believe a word of it."

Hog And Dog

A Jamaican Tale

This story has been adapted from Walter Jekyll's version that originally appeared in Jamaican Song and Story, published in 1904 by The Folk-lore Society & David Nutt, London.

One day, Hog, whose name was Cuddy, went out to look for work, but he couldn't find any. When he returned home, Rat hired him to keep watch for him while Brother Puss was approaching. Hog asked Rat about his pay, and Rat said he would give him three shillings and sixpence a week, but Hog had to provide his own food and drink. Hog didn't agree, but because times were tough, he decided to tolerate Rat until the end of the week.

When the week was over, Rat paid Hog, thinking that Hog was still keeping watch for him. So Rat went out, and when he returned, he didn't find Hog. He exclaimed that if it weren't for God, Puss would have caught him. He cursed Hog, saying that Hog would wander around and never find work, and that some people worse off than Hog would laugh at him.

One morning, Hog went out to look for work, and Mr. Dog, a market-keeper, saw him passing by. Dog asked Hog where he was going, and Hog replied that he was looking for some work. Dog burst into laughter and asked if Hog was still working for Rat. Hog felt so ashamed that he didn't answer Dog. Dog laughed at Hog and sang a mocking song until Hog became angry and returned home. Since that day, Hog has always hated Dog.

The Boy Who Was Changed into a Dog.

An Indian Tale

This tale is adapted from Folklore of the Santal Parganas, which is a collection of folklore from the Santal Parganas region, compiled by Cecil Henry Bompas and published by the Indian Civil Service in 1909. This work is significant for its detailed documentation of the oral traditions, myths, legends, and cultural practices of the Santal people, an indigenous ethnic group primarily located in the eastern part of India.

Once upon a time there were seven brothers. The six eldest were married, but the youngest was only a youth and looked after the cattle. The six married brothers spent their life in hunting and often used to be away from home for one or two months at a time. Now all their six wives were witches and directly their husbands left home the six women used to climb a peepul tree and ride away on it, to eat men or do some other devilry. The youngest brother saw them disappear every day and made up his mind to find out what they did.

So one morning he hid in a hollow in the trunk of the peepul tree and waited till his sisters-in-law came and climbed up into the branches. Then the tree rose up and was carried through the air to the banks of a large river, where the women climbed down and disappeared. After a time they came back and climbed into the tree and rode on it back to the place where it came from. But as they descended they saw their brother-in-law hiding in the trunk and at first they tried to make him promise not to tell what he had seen, but he swore that he would let his brothers know all about it. So then they thought of killing him, but in the end the eldest said that this was not necessary and she fetched two iron nails and drove them into the soles of his feet whereupon he at once became a dog. He could understand all that was said but of course could not speak. He followed them home and they treated him well and always gave him a regular helping at meals as if he were a human being and did not merely throw him the scraps as if he were a dog, nor would he have eaten them if they had.

A month afterwards the other brothers came home and asked if all had gone well in their absence. Their wives said that all was well except that the youngest brother had unfortunately disappeared without leaving any trace. While they were talking the dog came up and fawned on the brothers, so they asked where it had come from and the women said that it had followed them home on the day that they were looking for the missing boy, and they had kept it ever since. So matters rested. The brothers searched high and low but could not find the missing boy and so gave up the quest.

Now the Raja of that country had three daughters whom he had tried in vain to get married, but whenever a bridegroom was proposed to them they declared that he was not to their liking and they would have nothing to do with him. At last their father said that as they would not let him choose husbands for them, they must make the choice themselves. He proposed to assemble all the men in his kingdom on a certain day and there and then they must take to themselves husbands.

So proclamation was made that all the men were to assemble outside the palace and that three of them would receive the Raja's daughters in marriage without having to pay any bride price. On the fixed day a great crowd collected and among others went the six brothers, and the dog followed them. Then the three princesses were brought out and three flies were caught. Around one fly was tied a piece of white thread for the eldest princess and round the second fly a red thread for the second princess, and round the last fly a blue thread for the youngest princess. Then the three princesses solemnly promised that each would marry the man on whom the fly with her colour settled upon, and the flies were let loose. The red fly and the blue fly soon settled on two of the men sitting in the crowd but the white fly flew high in the air and circled round and at last settled on the dog which was sitting beside the six brothers.

At this the crowd laughed and jeered but the eldest princess said that she must accept what fate had decreed and that she would marry the dog. So the betrothal ceremony of the three princesses took place at once, soon followed by their weddings. The husbands of the two youngest princesses took their brides home, but the eldest princess stayed in her father's house with her dog.

One day after its dinner the dog was lying on its side asleep and the princess chanced to see the heads of the iron nails in its feet: "Ah," thought she, "that is why the poor dog limps." So she ran and fetched a pair of pincers and pulled out the nails. No sooner had she done so than the dog was restored to its human shape and the princess was delighted to find that not only was he a man but also very handsome, and they settled down to live happily together.

Some months later the six brothers resolved to go and visit the Raja, so that the princess might not feel that the dog she had married had no friends in the world. Off they set and when they reached the Raja's palace they were amazed to find their younger brother and still more so when they heard the story of all that had happened to him.

They immediately decided to take vengeance on their wives and when they reached home gave orders for a large well to be dug. When it was ready they told their wives to join in the consecration ceremony which was to ensure a pure and plentiful supply of water. So the six witches went to the well and while their attention was occupied, their husbands pushed them all into the well and filled it up with earth and that was the end of the witches.

The Dog And The Cock

A Russian Tale

This tale is adapted from More Russian Picture Tales, written and illustrated by Valery Carrick. The book was published by Frederick A. Stokes Co. in New York in 1914. This book is a collection of Russian folk tales specifically adapted for children, accompanied by charming illustrations that complement the stories.

One summer a certain peasant's crops failed him, and so he had no food to give to his animals, which were a cock and a dog. And the dog said to the cock, "Well, brother Peeter, I think we should get more to eat if we went and lived in the forest than here at our master's, don't you?"

"That's a fact," answered the cock, "let's be off."

So they said good-bye to their master and mistress and went off to see what they could find. And they went on and on, and couldn't find a nice place to stop. Then it began to grow dark, and the cock said, "Let's spend the night on a tree. I'll fly up on to a branch, and you take shelter in the hollow. We'll get through the night somehow."

So the cock made his way on to a branch, tucked in his toes, and went to sleep, while the dog made himself a bed in the hollow of the tree. And they slept soundly the whole night through, and towards morning, when it began to get light, the cock woke up and, as was his custom, crowed as loud as he could, "Cock-a-doodle-doo! cock-a-doodle-do! All wake up! All get up! The sun will soon be rising, and the day will soon begin!"

And he crowed so loudly, that a fox in a hole nearby was up in an instant thinking, "What a funny thing for a cock to be crowing in the forest! I expect he's lost his way and can't get out again!"

And he began to look for the cock, and after a bit he saw him sitting upon the branch of the tree. "Oh," thought the fox, "he'd make a fine meal! How can I get him to come down from there?"

So he went up to the tree and said to the cock: "What a splendid cock you are! I've never seen such a fine one all my days! What lovely feathers, just as if they were covered with gold! And your tail! nobody could describe it in words or on paper, it's so beautiful! And what a sweet voice you've got! I could listen to it all day and all night. Do fly down a little closer and let's get to know each other a little better. That reminds me, I've got a christening on at my place today, and I shall have plenty of food and drink to offer such a welcome guest. Let's go along to my home."

"Right you are," answered the cock, "I'll certainly come, only you must ask my companion too. We always go about together."

"And where is your companion?" asked the fox.

"Down below in the tree hollow," answered the cock. And the fox poked his head into the hole, thinking there was another cock there, when the dog popped his head out and caught Mr. Fox

The Dog And The Dog Dealer

An Indian Tale

This tale is adapted from The Junior Classics, Volume 1, edited by William Patten and published by P. F. Collier & Son in New York in 1912, which is part of a comprehensive anthology series aimed at children and young readers. This series, often referred to as "The Junior Classics," was designed to introduce young readers to a wide range of literature, including myths, legends, fairy tales, fables, and classic stories. This tale was originally told by Ramaswami Raju, also known as Pandit Ramaswami Raju, who was an Indian author and scholar known for his work in translating and compiling traditional Indian stories and folklore into English.

A dog was standing by the cottage of a peasant. A man who dealt in dogs passed by the way. The Dog said, "Will you buy me?"

The man said, "Oh, you ugly little thing! I would not give a quarter of a penny for you!"

Then the Dog went to the palace of the king and stood by the portal.

The sentinel caressed it, and said, "You are a charming little creature!"

Just then the Dog Dealer came by. The Dog said, "Will you buy me?"

"Oh," said the man, "you guard the palace of the king, who must have paid a high price for you. I cannot afford to pay the amount, else I would willingly take you."

"Ah!" said the Dog, "how place and position affect people!"

The Dog And The Moon

An Indigenous Aboriginal Tale From Australia

This tale is my own version of a traditional Australian Aboriginal myth. This tale originates from the Yolngu people of Arnhem Land in the Northern Territory.

The dog and the moon were once friends who lived together on Earth. However, the dog grew restless and longed to explore the sky like the moon. One day, the dog asked the moon if it could join him in the sky, but the moon refused, saying that there was no room for the dog in the heavens.

Undeterred, the dog persisted, pleading with the moon to allow him to ascend to the sky. Eventually, the moon relented but warned the dog that he must follow certain rules if he wished to stay in the sky.

The dog eagerly agreed and began his journey to the heavens. However, once he reached the sky, the dog became boastful and arrogant, disregarding the moon's warnings and causing chaos among the stars.

Angered by the dog's behaviour, the moon cast him out of the sky, condemning him to wander the Earth forever as a reminder of his folly. From that day forth, the dog became known as the "wandering dog" or "dingo," forever roaming the Australian outback in search of redemption.

The Dog And The Sparrow

A German Tale

This tale is adapted from Grimms' Fairy Tales, originally known as "Kinder- und Hausmärchen" (Children's and Household Tales), which is a collection of German folktales first published by Jacob and Wilhelm Grimm in 1812. The Grimm brothers were German academics, linguists, and cultural researchers who sought to preserve the folklore of their country.

A shepherd's dog had a master who took no care of him, but often let him suffer the greatest hunger. At last he could bear it no longer. so he took to his heels, and off he ran in a very sad and sorrowful mood.

On the road he met a sparrow that said to him, "Why are you so sad, my friend?"

"Because," said the dog, "I am very, very hungry, and have nothing to eat."

"If that be all," answered the sparrow, "come with me into the next town, and I will soon find you plenty of food."

So on they went together into the town: and as they passed by a butcher's shop, the sparrow said to the dog, "Stand there a little while till I peck you down a piece of meat."

So the sparrow perched upon the shelf, and having first looked carefully about her to see if anyone was watching her, she pecked and scratched at a steak that lay upon the edge of the shelf, till at last down it fell. Then the dog snapped it up, and scrambled away with it into a corner, where he soon ate it all up.

"Well," said the sparrow, "you shall have some more if you want, so come with me to the next shop, and I will peck you down another steak."

When the dog had eaten this too, the sparrow said to him, "Well, my good friend, have you had enough now?"

"I have had plenty of meat," answered he, "but I should like to have a piece of bread to eat after it."

"Come with me then," said the sparrow, "and you shall soon have that too."

So she took him to a baker's shop, and pecked at two rolls that lay in the window, till they fell down, and as the dog still wished for more, she took him to another shop and pecked down some more for him. When that was eaten, the sparrow asked him whether he had had enough now.

"Yes," said he, "and now let us take a walk a little way out of the town."

So they both went out upon the high road, but as the weather was warm, they had not gone far before the dog said, "I am very tired. I should like to take a nap."

"Very well," answered the sparrow, "do so, and in the meantime I will perch upon that bush."

So the dog stretched himself out on the road, and fell fast asleep. Whilst he slept, there came by a carter with a cart drawn by three horses, and loaded with two casks of wine. The sparrow, seeing that the carter did not turn out of the way, but would go on in the track in which the dog lay, so as to drive over him, called out, "Stop! Stop, Mr Carter, or it shall be the worse for you."

But the carter, grumbling to himself, said "You make it the worse for me, indeed! what can you do?"

He cracked his whip, and drove his cart over the poor dog, so that the wheels crushed him to death.

"There," cried the sparrow, "you cruel villain, you have killed my friend the dog. Now mind what I say. This deed of yours shall cost you all you are worth."

"Do your worst, and welcome," said the brute. 'What harm can you do me?"

But the sparrow crept under the tilt of the cart, and pecked at the bung of one of the casks till she loosened it, and then all the wine ran out, without the carter seeing it.

At last he looked round, and saw that the cart was dripping, and the cask quite empty. "What an unlucky wretch I am!" cried he.

"Not wretch enough yet!" said the sparrow, as she alighted upon the head of one of the horses, and pecked at him till he reared up and kicked. When the carter saw this, he drew out his hatchet and aimed a blow at the sparrow, meaning to kill her, but she flew away, and the blow fell upon the poor horse's head with such force, that he fell down dead.

"Unlucky wretch that I am!" cried he.

"Not wretch enough yet!" said the sparrow.

And as the carter went on with the other two horses, she again crept under the tilt of the cart, and pecked out the bung of the second cask, so that all the wine ran out. When the carter saw this, he again cried out, "Miserable wretch that I am!"

But the sparrow answered, "Not wretch enough yet!" and perched on the head of the second horse, and pecked at him too. The carter ran up and struck at her again with his hatchet, but away she flew, and the blow fell upon the second horse and killed him on the spot.

"Unlucky wretch that I am!" said he.

"Not wretch enough yet!" said the sparrow, and perching upon the third horse, she began to peck him too. The carter was mad with fury, and without looking about him, or caring what he was about, struck again at the sparrow, but killed his third horse as he done the other two.

"Alas! Miserable wretch that I am!" cried he.

"Not wretch enough yet!" answered the sparrow as she flew away. "Now I will plague and punish you at your own house."

The carter was forced at last to leave his cart behind him, and to go home overflowing with rage and vexation. "Alas!" said he to his wife, "What ill luck has befallen me! My wine is all spilt, and my horses are dead."

"Alas, husband," replied she, "and a wicked bird has come into the house, and has brought with her all the birds in the world, I am sure, and they have fallen upon our corn in the loft, and are eating it up at such a rate!"

Away ran the husband upstairs, and saw thousands of birds sitting upon the floor eating up his corn, with the sparrow in the midst of them.

"Unlucky wretch that I am!" cried the carter; for he saw that the corn was almost all gone.

"Not wretch enough yet!" said the sparrow; "your cruelty shall cost you your life yet!' and away she flew.

The carter seeing that he had thus lost all that he had, went down into his kitchen, and was still not sorry for what he had done, but sat himself angrily and sulkily in the chimney corner.

But the sparrow sat on the outside of the window, and cried 'Carter! Your cruelty shall cost you your life!"

With that he jumped up in a rage, seized his hatchet, and threw it at the sparrow, but it missed her, and only broke the window. The sparrow now hopped in, perched upon the window-seat, and cried, "Carter! It shall cost you your life!"

Then he became mad and blind with rage, and struck the window-seat with such force that he cleft it in two: and as the sparrow flew from place to place, the carter and his wife were so furious, that they broke all their furniture, glasses, chairs, benches, the table, and at last the walls, without touching the bird at all.

In the end, however, they caught her: and the wife said, "Shall I kill her at once?"

"No," cried he, "that is letting her off too easily. She shall die a much crueller death. I will eat her."

But the sparrow began to flutter about, and stretch out her neck and cried, "Carter! it shall cost you your life yet!"

With that he could wait no longer, so he gave his wife the hatchet, and cried, "Wife, strike at the bird and kill her in my hand."

And the wife struck, but she missed her aim, and hit her husband on the head so that he fell down dead, and the sparrow flew quietly home to her nest.

The Dog Fanti

A Scottish Tale

This tale is adapted from Andrew Lang's book, The Book of Dreams and Ghosts, published by Longmans, Green and Co. in London and New York in 1899. The book is a fascinating exploration of supernatural phenomena, particularly focusing on dreams and ghostly encounters. Lang, a prolific author and folklorist, compiled a wide range of stories and accounts that delve into the mysterious and the otherworldly.

Mrs. Ogilvie of Drumquaigh had a poodle named Fanti. Her family, or at least those who lived with her, were her son, the laird, and three daughters. Of these the two younger, at a certain recent date, were paying a short visit to a neighbouring country house.

Mrs. Ogilvie was accustomed to breakfast in her bedroom, not being in the best of health. One morning her daughter came down to breakfast and said to her brother, "I had an odd dream; I dreamed Fanti went mad".

"Well, that is odd," said her brother. "So did I. We had better not tell mother as it might make her nervous."

Miss Ogilvie went up after breakfast to see the elder lady, who said, "Do turn out Fanti. I dreamed last night that he went mad and bit".

In the afternoon the two younger sisters came home.

"How did you enjoy yourselves?" one of the others asked.

"We didn't sleep well. I was dreaming that Fanti went mad when Mary wakened me, and said she had dreamed Fanti went mad, and turned into a cat, and we threw him into the fire."

Macphie's Black Dog

A Scottish Tale

This story has been adapted from a tale told in Gaelic by Donald Cameron and translated by John Gregorson Campbell that appeared in Superstitions of the Highlands and Islands of Scotland, published in 1900 by James MacLehose and Sons, publishers to Glasgow University.

Mac-vic-Allan of Arasaig, lord of Moidart, went out hunting in his own forest when young and unmarried. He saw a royal stag before him, as beautiful an animal as he had ever seen. He levelled his gun at it, and it suddenly became a woman as beautiful as he had ever seen at all. He lowered his gun, and it became a royal stag as before.

Every time he raised the gun to his eye, the figure was that of a woman, and every time he let it down to the ground, it was a royal stag. Upon this he raised the gun to his eye and walked up till he was close to the woman's breast. He then sprang and caught her in his arms.

"You will not be separated from me at all," he said, "I will never marry any but you."

"Do not do that, Mac-vic-Allan," she said, "you have no business with me, I will not suit you. There will never be a day, while you have me with you, but you will need to kill a cow for me."

"You will get that," said the lord of Moidart, "even if you should ask two a day."

But Mac-vic-Allan's herd began to grow thin, so eventually he tried to send her away, but he could not. He then went to an old man, who lived in the townland, and was his counsellor. He said he would be a broken man, and he did not know what plan to take to get rid of her. The honest old man told him, that unless Macphie of Colonsay could send her away, there was not another living who could. A letter was instantly sent off to Macphie., and he answered the letter, and came to Arasaig.

"What business is this you have with me, Mac-vic-Allan?" said Macphie.

Mac-vic-Allan told him how the woman had come upon him, and how he could not send her away.

"Go" said Macphie, "and kill a cow for her today as usual. Send her dinner to the room as usual, and give me my dinner on the other side of the room."

Mac-vic-Allan did as he was asked. She commenced her dinner, and Macphie commenced his. When Macphie finished his dinner, he looked over at her.

"What is your news, Elle-maid?" said he.

"What is that to you, Brian Brugh," said she.

"I saw you, Elle-maid," said he, "when you consorted with the Fingalians, and when you went with Dermid o Duvne and accompanied him from covert to covert."

"I saw you, Brian Brugh," she said, "when you rode on an old black horse, the lover of the slim Fairy woman, Ever chasing her from brugh to brugh."

With that, the woman ran from the house.

"Dogs and men after the wretch," cried Macphie, "long have I known her."

Every dog and man in Arasaig was called and sent after her. She fled away out to the point of Arasaig, and they did not get a second sight of her.

With this task done, Macphie went home to his own Colonsay. One day he was out hunting, and night came on before he got home. He saw a light and made straight for it. He saw a number of men sitting in there, and an old grey-headed man in the midst. The old man spoke and said, "Macphie, come forward."

Macphie went forward, and what should come in his way but a bitch, as beautiful an animal as he had ever seen, and a litter of pups with it. He saw one pup in particular, black in colour, and he had never seen a pup so black or so beautiful as it.

"This dog will be my own," said Macphie.

"No," said the man, "you will get your choice of the pups, but you will not get that one."

"I will not take one," said Macphie, "but this one."

"Since you are resolved to have it," said the old man, "it will not do you but one day's service, and it will do that well. Come back on such a night and you will get it."

Macphie reached the place on the night he promised to come. They gave him the dog, "and take care of it well," said the old man, "for it will never do service for you but the one day."

The Black Dog began to turn out so handsome a whelp that no one ever saw a dog so large or so beautiful as it. When Macphie went out hunting he called the Black Dog, and the Black Dog came to the door and then turned back and lay where it was before. The gentlemen who visited at Macphie's house used to tell him to kill the

Black Dog, it was not worth its food. Macphie would tell them to let the dog alone, that the Black Dog's day would come yet.

At one time a number of gentlemen came across from Islay to visit Macphie and ask him to go with them to Jura to hunt. At that time Jura was a desert, without anyone staying on it, and without its equal anywhere as hunting ground for deer and roe. There was a place there where those who went for sport used to stay, called the Big Cave. A boat was made ready to cross the sound that same day. Macphie rose to go with the sixteen young gentlemen Each of them called the Black Dog, and it reached the door, then turned and lay down where it was before.

"Shoot it," cried the young gentlemen.

"No," said he, "the Black Dog's day has not come yet"

They reached the shore, but the wind rose and they did not get across that day.

Next day they made ready to go. The Black Dog was called and reached the door, but returned where it was before.

"Kill it," said the gentlemen, "and don't be feeding it any longer."

"I will not kill it," said Macphie, "the Black Dog's day will come yet."

They failed to get across this day also from the violence of the weather and returned.

"The dog has foreknowledge," said the gentlemen.

"It has foreknowledge," said Macphie, "that its own day will come yet."

On the third day the weather was beautiful. They took their way to the harbour, and did not say a syllable this day to the Black Dog. They launched the boat to go away, when one of the gentlemen looked and said the Black Dog was coming, and he never saw a creature like it, because of its fierce look. It sprang, and was the first creature in the boat.

"The Black Dog's day is drawing near us," said Macphie.

They took with them meat, and provisions, and bedclothes, and went ashore in Jura. They passed that night in the Big Cave, and next day went to hunt the deer. Late in the evening they came home. They prepared supper. They had a fine fire in the cave and light. There was a big hole in the very roof of the cave through which a man could pass. When they had taken their supper the young gentlemen lay down, Macphie rose, and stood warming the back of his legs to the fire. Each of the young men said he wished his own sweetheart was there that night.

"Well," said Macphie, "I prefer that my wife should be in her own house. It is enough for me to be here myself tonight."

Macphie then saw sixteen women entering the door of the cave. The light went out and there was no light except what the fire gave. The women went over to where the gentlemen were. Macphie could see nothing from the darkness that came over the cave. He was not hearing a sound from the men. The women stood up and one of them looked at Macphie. She stood opposite him as though she were going to attack him. The Black Dog rose and bristled fiercely and sprang at her. The women took to the door, and the Black Dog followed them to the mouth of the cave. When they went away the Black Dog returned and lay at Macphie's feet.

In a little while Macphie heard a horrid noise overhead in the top of the cave, so that he thought the cave would fall in about his head. He looked up and saw a man's hand coming down through the hole, and looking like the hand wanted to catch Macphie and take him out through the hole in the roof of the cave. The Black Dog gave one spring, and between the shoulder and the elbow caught the Hand, and lay upon it with all its might.

Now began the play between the Hand and the Black Dog. Before the Black Dog let go its hold, it chewed the arm through till it fell on the floor. The Thing that was on the top of the cave went away, and Macphie thought the cave would fall in about his head. The Black Dog rushed out after the Thing that was outside. When the day dawned, the Black Dog returned. It lay down at Macphie's feet, and in a few minutes was dead.

When the light of day appeared Macphie looked, and none of his companions were alive. He took the Hand, and went to the boat. He went on board and went home to Colonsay, unaccompanied by dog or man. He took the Hand with him so that men might see the horror he had met in the cave. No man in Islay or Colonsay ever at all saw such a hand, nor did they imagine that such existed. There only remained to send a boat to Jura and take home the bodies that were in the cave. That was the end of the Black Dog's day.

Dog Tails – Canine Fairy Tales, Myths And Legends

The Dog O' Mause

A Scottish Tale

This tale is adapted from Andrew Lang's book, The Book of Dreams and Ghosts, published by Longmans, Green and Co. in London and New York in 1899. The book is a fascinating exploration of supernatural phenomena, particularly focusing on dreams and ghostly encounters. Lang, a prolific author and folklorist, compiled a wide range of stories and accounts that delve into the mysterious and the otherworldly.

This is a written account of an apparition that appeared to William Soutar in the Mause in 1730:

"I have sent you an account of an apparition as remarkable, perhaps, as anything you ever heard of, and which, considered in all its circumstances, leaves, I think, no ground of doubt to any man of common-sense. The person to whom it appeared is one William Soutar, a tenant of Balgowan's, who lives in Middle Mause, within about half a mile from this place on the other side of the river, and in view from our windows of Craighall House. He is about thirty-seven years of age, as he says, and has a wife and bairns.

"The following is an account from his own mouth, and because there are some circumstances fit to be taken in as you go along, I have given them with reference at the end, that I may not interrupt the sense of the account, or add anything to it. Therefore, it begins:

"In the month of December in the year 1728, about sky-setting, I and my servant, with several others living in the farm-steading heard a scratching, a screeching, and a crying, and I followed the noise, with my servant, a little way from the farm-steading. We both thought we saw what had the appearance to be a fox, and hounded the dogs at it, but they would not pursue it.

"About a month after, as I was coming from Blair alone, about the same time of the night, a big dog appeared to me, of a dark greyish colour, between the Hilltown and Knockhead of Mause, on a lea rig a little below the road, and in passing by it touched me firmly on the thigh at my hip-bone, upon which I pulled my staff from under my arm and let a stroke at it, and I had a notion at the time that I hit it, and my hip was painful all that night. However, I had no great thought of its being anything particular or extraordinary, but that it might be a mad dog wandering. About a year after that, to the best of my memory, in December, about the same time of the night and in the same place, when I was alone, it appeared to me again as before, and passed by me at some distance, and then I began to think it might be something more than ordinary.

"In the month of December 1730, as I was coming from Perth, from the Claith Market a little before sky-setting, it appeared to me again, being alone, at the same place, and passed by me just as before. I had some suspicion of it then likewise, but I began to think that a neighbour of mine in the Hilltown having an ox lately dead, it might be a dog that had been at the carrion, by which I endeavoured to put the suspicion out of my head.

"On the second Monday of December 1730, as I was coming from Woodhead, a farm in the ground of Drumlochy, it appeared to me again in the same place just about sky-setting, and after it had passed me as it was going out of my sight, it spoke with a low voice so that I distinctly heard it say, 'Within eight or ten days do or die,' and it thereupon disappeared.

No more passed at that time. On the morrow I went to my brother, who dwells in the Nether Aird of Drumlochy, and told him of the last and of all the former appearances, which was the first time I ever spoke of it to anybody. He and I went to see a sister of ours at Glenballow, who was dying, but she was dead before we came. As we were returning home, I desired my brother, whose name is James Soutar, to go forward with me till we should be passed the place where the dog used to appear to me, and just as we had come to it, about ten o'clock at night, it appeared to me again just as formerly, and as it was passing over some ice I pointed to it with my finger and asked my brother if he saw it, but he said he did not, nor did his servant, who was with us. It spoke nothing at that time, but just disappeared as it passed the ice.

"On the Saturday after, as I was at my own sheep-cots putting in my sheep, it appeared to me again just after daylight, between day and skylight, and upon saying these words, 'Come to the spot of ground within half an hour,' it just disappeared. I came home to my own house, and took up a staff and also a sword off the head of the bed, and went straight to the place where it used formerly to appear to me, and after I had been there some minutes and had drawn a circle about me with my staff, it appeared to me.

I spoke to it saying, 'In the name of God and Jesus Christ, what are you that troubles me?'

"It answered me, 'I am David Soutar, George Soutar's brother. I killed a man more than five-and-thirty years ago, when you was newborn, at a bush be-east the road, as you go into the Isle.'

"And as I was going away, I stood again and said, 'David Soutar was a man, and you appear like a dog.'

"It spoke to me again, saying, 'I killed him with a dog, and therefore I am made to speak out of the mouth of a dog, and tell you that you must go and bury these bones'.

"Upon this I went straight to my brother to his house, and told him what had happened to me. My brother told the minister of Blair, and we went to the minister on Monday thereafter, as he was examining in a neighbour's house in the same town where I live. And the minister, with my brother and me and two or three more, went to the place where the apparition said the bones were buried, when Rychalzie met us accidentally, and the minister told Rychalzie the story in the presence of all that were there assembled, and desired the liberty from him to break up the ground to search for the bones. Rychalzie made some scruples to allow us to break up the ground, but said he would go along with us to Glasclune, and if he advised, he would allow search to be made. Accordingly he went straight along with my brother and me and James Chalmers, a neighbour who lives in the Hilltown of Mause, to Glasclune, and told Glasclune the story as above narrated, and he advised Rychalzie to allow the search to be made, whereupon he gave his consent to it.

"The day after, being Friday, we convened about thirty or forty men and went to the Isle, and broke up the ground in many places, searching for the bones, but we found nothing.

"On Wednesday the 23rd December, about twelve o'clock, when I was in my bed, I heard a voice but saw nothing. The voice said, 'Come away'.

"Upon this I rose out of my bed, cast on my coat and went to the door, but did not see it. And I said, 'In the name of God, what do you demand of me now?'

"It answered, 'Go, take up these bones'.

"I said, 'How shall I get these bones?'

"It answered again, 'At the side of a withered bush, and there are but seven or eight of them remaining'.

"I asked, 'Was there any more guilty of that action but you?'

"It answered, 'No'.

"I asked again, 'What is the reason you trouble me?'

"It answered, 'Because you are the youngest'.

"Then said I to it, 'Depart from me, and give me a sign that I may know the particular spot, and give me time'.

"'You will find the bones at the side of a withered bush. There are but eight of them, and for a sign you will find the print of a cross impressed on the ground.'

"On the morrow, being Thursday, I went alone to the Isle to see if I could find any sign, and immediately I saw both the bush, which was a small bush, the greatest stick in it being about the thickness of a staff, and it was withered about half-way down, and also the sign, which was about a foot from the bush. The sign was an exact cross, each of the two lines was about a foot and a half in length and near three inches broad, and more than an inch deeper than the rest of the ground, as if it had been pressed down, for the ground was not cut.

"On the morrow, being Friday, I went and told my brother of the voice that had spoken to me, and that I had gone and seen the bush which it directed me to and the above-mentioned sign there. The next day, being Saturday, my brother and I went, together with seven or eight men with us, to the Isle. About sun-rising we all saw the bush and the sign, and upon breaking up the ground just at the bush, we found the bones. They were the chaft-teeth, one of the thigh bones, one of the shoulder blades, and a small bone which we supposed to be a collar bone, which was more consumed than any of the rest, and two other small bones, which we thought to be bones of the sword-arm. By the time we had dug up those bones, there convened about forty men who also saw them. The minister and Rychalzie came to the place and saw them.

"'We immediately sent to the other side of the water, to Claywhat, to a wright that was cutting timber there, whom Claywhat brought over with him, who immediately made a coffin for the bones, and my wife brought linen to wrap them in, and I wrapped the bones in the linen myself and put them in the coffin before all these people, and sent for the mort-cloth and buried them in the churchyard of Blair that evening. There were near a hundred persons at the burial, and it was a little after sunset when they were buried."

Dog Tails – Canine Fairy Tales, Myths And Legends

Why Dogs Sniff

A Portuguese Tale

This story has been adapted from an anonymous original translated by Elsie Spicer Eells that appeared in The Islands Of Magic, Legends, Folk And Fairy Tales From The Azores, published in 1922 Harcourt, Brace And Company, New York.

Once upon a time the dogs gave a dinner party. All the dogs were invited and all the dogs accepted the invitation. There were big dogs and little dogs and middle-sized dogs. There were black dogs and white dogs and brown dogs and grey dogs and yellow dogs and spotted dogs. There were dogs with long tails and dogs with short tails and dogs with no tails at all. There were dogs with little sharp-pointed ears and dogs with big flat drooping ears. There were dogs with long slender noses and dogs with short fat turn-up noses. All these dogs came to the party.

Now the dinner was a most elaborate affair. Everything had been arranged with the utmost care. All the good things to eat were spread out upon the rocks by the sea. A gay sparkling little brook brought water to drink. The sun was shining brightly and a soft gentle little breeze was blowing. Everything seemed absolutely perfect.

But there was a cross fussy old dog who came to the party. She was a yellow dog, they say. Nothing ever suited her. Whenever she went to a party she always found fault with something. Sometimes there was too little to eat and sometimes there was too much. Sometimes the hot things were not hot enough and sometimes the cold things were not cold enough. Sometimes the hot things were so hot they burned her mouth and the cold things so cold that they gave her indigestion. There was always something wrong.

At this party, however, there was not too much to eat and there was not too little to eat. The hot things were all just hot enough and the cold things were all just cold enough. Everything seemed to be exactly as it should be.

"How good everything tastes!" remarked the big black dog between polite mouthfuls.

"Everything is seasoned exactly right," added the black and white spotted dog between mouthfuls which were entirely too large to be polite.

That was an unfortunate remark. The cross fussy yellow dog heard it. She noticed immediately that the big juicy bone she was eating had not been seasoned with pepper.

"Will somebody please pass the pepper?" she asked.

All the black dogs and white dogs and brown dogs and yellow dogs and grey dogs and spotted dogs fell over each other trying to find the pepper to pass. There was not a single bit of pepper at that dinner party.

"I can't eat a mouthful until I have some pepper," whined the yellow dog.

"I'll go into the city and get some pepper," said one of the dogs. Nobody ever knew which dog it was.

The dog who went into the city to get the pepper never came back. Nobody ever knew what became of him.

Whenever two dogs meet they always sniff at each other. If one of them should happen to be the dog who went into the city to get the pepper, he would surely smell of pepper.

The Dog's Trial

A Finnish Tale

This tale is adapted from Eero Salmelainen's book Fairy Tales and Stories of the Finnish People, published by the Finnish Literary Society in 1852, which is a pivotal work in the documentation and celebration of Finnish folklore, reflecting the rich oral traditions and cultural heritage of Finland. It remains a valuable resource for understanding the nation's literary and cultural history.

Muuda's owner did not feed his dog well. He only gave it bones and the small breadcrumbs left at the table by people. The dog was unhappy with this and decided to complain to the court. He presented his case, explaining how poorly his owner treated him. The court then ruled in the dog's favour and declared, "Your master must provide you with a soft pillow to lie on in the summer, a woollen blanket in the winter, and bread and meat to eat."

Satisfied with this decision, the dog headed home, determined to remember the court's ruling. Along the way, he met a fox who asked where he had been and what he was doing. The dog explained his trip to the court, his complaint, and the favourable judgment he had received. The fox was delighted to hear that the dog had won his case and was eager to hear more about the court's decision and other details.

As they talked, the dog became so engrossed in the conversation that he forgot the specifics of the court's decision. Eventually, as they were about to part ways, the dog asked the fox in frustration, "What exactly did the court decide again?"

The fox replied, "You told me that the court ordered your owner to continue giving you bones and burnt bread crusts as food, to let you lie on chips in the summer, and on a snowdrift in the winter."

Hearing this, the dog realized he had misunderstood the court's decision. He walked home in a bad mood, feeling no better off than before.

The Black Dogs

A Cornish Tale

This story has been adapted from an original collected by Robert Hunt that appeared in Popular Romances of the West of England, published in 1865 by Camden Hotten, Piccadilly, London.

Around thirty years ago, a man and a boy were working on sinking a shaft at Wheal Vor Mine. During their work, the boy either carelessly or accidentally made a mistake while charging a hole with explosives. This mistake made it necessary to perform the dangerous task of removing the faulty charge. As they began this delicate operation, the man sternly reprimanded the boy for his carelessness. Meanwhile, several other miners were preparing to change their shift and were on the platform above, occasionally calling down and conversing with the man and boy below.

Suddenly, the charge exploded. The man and boy were seen being hurled upward amidst a burst of flames. Rescue efforts were immediately undertaken, and a team quickly descended into the shaft. When they reached the bottom, they found the remains of the unfortunate pair, which were so badly shattered and scorched that they were unrecognizable. When the bodies were brought to the surface, their clothes and mangled flesh fell away.

To spare the families from the horrific sight, a bystander quickly gathered the gruesome remains with a shovel and threw them into the blazing furnace of Woolf's engine, which was nearby. Since that tragic incident, the engine operators claimed that they were continually haunted by the presence of small black dogs, which appeared even when the doors were shut. Although few liked to talk about it, the haunting presence made it difficult to find workers willing to operate the machine.

The Guilty Dogs

A Tibetan Tale

F. Anton von Schiefner's book Tibetan Tales, published by Kegan Paul, Trench, Trubner & Co. Ltd. in London in 1906, is an essential work for anyone interested in Tibetan folklore, providing a window into the rich narrative traditions of Tibet and reflecting the scholarly rigour of its translator.

In long-past times, King Brahmadatta came to the throne in Vārāṇasī, at a period when the land was blessed with riches, profusion, prosperity, and crops, and had a large population. Now there were two dogs, Gaṇḍa and Upagaṇḍa by name, which used to gnaw the king's horse-gear. Once when King Brahmadatta was going to take the field against the Licchavis, he ordered his ministers to inspect the horse-gear. When they had done this, and found that it was all torn and tattered, they said to the king, "O king, the dogs have gnawed the horse-gear to pieces."

The king said, "Honoured sirs, if this is the case, I give up the dogs altogether."

Thereupon some of them were killed and others ran away. A dog, which came from another country, seeing them running off, asked them what had frightened them so much. They gave a full account of all that had occurred. It said, "Why do not you implore the king for mercy?"

They replied, "We who are running away have no power of imploring the king, and the others have been rendered mute."

The other dog said, "Wait awhile, I will speak with the king on your behalf."

Encouraged by him they turned back, and after they had made a halt the three dogs expressed their prayer in a verse, uttered at a distance from which they could be heard, saying:

"These two dogs, Gaṇḍa and Upagaṇḍa,

full of force and health,

living in the king's stronghold,

ought to be put to death.

We are not deserving of death.

O king, it is not right to let

the innocent be put to death."

Having heard this, the king said next day to his ministers, "Honoured sirs, find out those who implored me yesterday in verse."

The ministers gave orders to the body-guards, saying, "Find out those who implored the king yesterday in verse."

The guards said, "It was the dogs of the land that did so."

The king said, "Honoured sirs, find out whether the horse-gear was devoured by Gaṇḍa and Upagaṇḍa, or by other dogs."

The ministers assembled, and began to take counsel together, saying, "Honoured sirs, the king has ordered us to find out about the dogs. How shall we manage it?"

Then some of them said, "There is only one way of finding out. The dogs must be given a hair-pellet and made to vomit."

When the pellet of hair had been given to the dogs, and they had been made to vomit, Gaṇḍa and Upagaṇḍa brought up fragments of leather. When the king had been informed of this, he delivered those dogs over to death. But he rendered the others free from fear.

The Legend Of Artemis

A Greek Tale

This tale is my own version of a traditional Greek myth.

Artemis, the goddess of the hunt, was renowned throughout the ancient world for her skill with a bow and arrow. But she was not alone in her pursuit of game. Accompanying her on her hunts were a pack of loyal hounds, fierce and swift creatures bred for the chase.

Artemis' favourite hound was named Sirius, a magnificent creature with sleek fur and keen senses. Sirius was not just any ordinary dog, for he was gifted with extraordinary speed and strength, traits bestowed upon him by the goddess herself.

Together with Sirius and her other faithful hounds, Artemis would venture deep into the forests and mountains, tracking her quarry with unmatched precision. With her bow in hand and her hounds at her side, she was a force to be reckoned with, feared by all manner of game.

But Artemis was not just a hunter. She was also a protector of the wild places. She respected the balance of nature and took only what she needed for sustenance, never hunting for sport or pleasure alone.

On one memorable hunt, Artemis and her hounds pursued a mighty stag through the dense forest. The beast was swift and elusive, leading them on a wild chase through the underbrush. But Artemis and her hounds were relentless, their determination unwavering.

As they closed in on their quarry, the stag made one final desperate attempt to escape, darting into a thicket of thorns. But Artemis and Sirius were undeterred. With a swift motion, Artemis drew her bow and let loose an arrow, striking the stag true.

As the mighty beast fell, Artemis approached it with reverence, thanking the gods for the bounty they had provided. She and her hounds would feast well that night, but they would also honour the spirit of the fallen stag, offering prayers for its soul to find peace in the afterlife.

And so, Artemis continued her hunts, roaming the wild places of the world with her faithful hounds by her side. Together, they were a formidable team, embodying the spirit of the hunt and the untamed beauty of the natural world.

The Man And The Water-Dogs

An Arikara Tale

This tale is adapted from George Amos Dorsey's book "Traditions of the Arikara," published by the Carnegie Institution of Washington in 1904, This book is an important ethnographic work that documents the folklore, traditions, and cultural practices of the Arikara people, a Native American tribe.

Long ago there was a village with so many inhabitants that it had four medicine-lodges. There was one man who was so brave that his fame extended beyond the village. He committed some evil deeds among his own people, but his people were afraid to correct him, and so he went on, committing more misdemeanours.

He became so bad that the people undertook to take his life. They formed a plot to seize him. One family invited the man to a feast. When he entered the lodge many men gathered about the lodge and waited till he came out. The man came out and walked very slowly toward the river. He paid no attention to the men nor even tried to fight back, but went on his way. Finally he stepped into the river, and someone cried out to the men to catch him, but it was too late. He sank down in the water and the people shouted for joy, because they thought he was drowned.

The man walked on down on the bottom of the river and he saw there a tipi. From its door came a Dog, and the Dog called to the man to come in. He went in, and he saw many Dogs. The leader of the Dogs raised his head and said that he was not hurt and that they never would injure him. The leader showed much mercy toward the man and told him not to be afraid of any man, and that if he should ever get hurt he was to come right to the water and the Dogs would be glad to receive him. So the man went out of the tipi and came up out of the water. When it was night he went to the village.

He entered his house and saw his wife. He sat down and told her that he regarded as nothing all the wounds he had received from the men who tried to kill him. The woman was surprised, and was much afraid of him. The man ordered his wife to go after some tobacco from one of the councils that was being held in the village. She went at once and entered one of the councils. She asked the head men for some tobacco for her husband. The men were much agitated and afraid, so they gave her some tobacco. The woman returned and the man was much pleased. The men in the council decided to send a messenger to see if the man had returned. One young man went and peeped in and saw the man, all naked, sitting in his tipi. He returned to the council and told what he had seen. The men were more afraid.

From that time on, the man committed worse crimes than before, yet the people were afraid to make another attempt to kill him. The man's relatives gathered with the woman's relatives and they separated from the village, to return no more. They went in the night, and before morning they camped. Some young men and the famous one came to the village and killed a man and a woman. The people knew who it was and yet they did not dare to fight them. This was a separation where the people never meet again, which happened because the man did the bad deeds.

Church Grim

An English Tale

This tale is my own version of a traditional English legend that probably has its roots in old Saxon and Norse storytelling.

Long ago, in a quaint English village nestled amidst rolling hills and ancient forests, there stood a small stone church with a weathered spire that reached toward the heavens. This church was not only a place of worship but also a sanctuary for the souls of the departed.

Legend had it that every church had a guardian spirit known as the Church Grim, a spectral dog tasked with protecting the sacred grounds from evil spirits and malevolent forces. It was said that the Church Grim would roam the churchyard at night, keeping watch over the graves and ensuring that the souls resting peacefully within were undisturbed.

In this particular village, there lived a young blacksmith named Jack, known for his kindness and bravery. Jack had heard the stories of the Church Grim since he was a child, but he had never encountered the spectral guardian himself.

One moonlit night, as Jack was returning home from his forge, he heard a mournful howling echoing through the churchyard. Curious, he followed the sound until he reached the old stone church. There, under the pale glow of the moon, he saw a large black dog with glowing eyes standing among the tombstones.

Jack's heart raced as he realized he was face to face with the Church Grim. The spectral dog regarded him with an inscrutable gaze, its eyes filled with ancient wisdom and solemn duty.

"Who goes there?" the Church Grim spoke in a deep, rumbling voice that seemed to emanate from the very earth itself.

"It is I, Jack the blacksmith," he replied, trying to keep his voice steady despite his fear. "I mean no harm, noble guardian. I only seek to pay my respects to the departed."

The Church Grim regarded Jack for a long moment before nodding in acknowledgment. "You show courage and respect, young blacksmith," it said. "Few mortals dare to venture into the realm of the dead."

Jack felt a surge of pride at the compliment from the spectral guardian. Emboldened, he approached the Church Grim and extended a hand in friendship. To his surprise, the spectral dog nuzzled his hand, its fur cold to the touch yet comforting in its presence.

From that night on, Jack and the Church Grim became unlikely companions, bound by a mutual respect and understanding. Together, they patrolled the churchyard, keeping watch over the graves and ensuring that the departed souls could rest in peace.

As the years passed, Jack grew old, and his hair turned silver, but his friendship with the Church Grim remained steadfast. And when the time came for Jack to join the souls of the departed, it was the Church Grim who escorted him to his final resting place, standing vigil by his grave until the end of time.

And so, the legend of the Church Grim lived on, a testament to the enduring bond between mortal and spirit, guardian and protector, in the eternal dance between the living and the dead.

The Orphan Boy And The Hell-Hounds

An Estonian Tale

William Forsell Kirby's book "The Hero of Esthonia and Other Studies in the Romantic Literature of That Country," published by John C. Nimmo in London in 1895, is an important work that delves into the folklore, mythology, and romantic literature of Estonia.

Once upon a time there lived a poor labourer and his wife, who dragged on a wretched existence from day to day. They had three children, but only the youngest survived. He was a boy of nine years old when he buried first his father and then his mother, and he had no other resource than to beg his bread from door to door. A year afterwards he happened to come to the house of a rich farmer just when they wanted a herd boy. The farmer himself was not such a bad man to deal with, but his wife had control of everything, and she was a regular brute. It may easily be imagined how much the poor orphan boy suffered. The blows that he received daily were three times more than sufficient, but he never got enough bread to eat. But as the orphan had nothing better to look forward to, he was forced to endure his misery.

One day the poor boy had the misfortune to lose a cow from the herd. He ran about the forest till sundown from one place to another, but could not find the lost cow, and although he well knew what awaited him when he reached home, he was at last obliged to gather the herd together without the missing cow. The sun had not long set when he heard the voice of his mistress shouting, "You lazy dog, where are you dawdling with the herd?" He could not wait longer, but was forced to hurry home to the stick. It was already growing dusk when the herd arrived at the gate, but the sharp eyes of the mistress had already discovered that one cow was missing. Without saying a word, she snatched the first stake from the fence, and began to belabour the boy, as if she would beat him to a jelly. She was in such a rage that she would certainly have beaten him to death, or made him a cripple for life, if the farmer, hearing his cries and sobs, had not compassionately come to his aid.

But as he knew the temper of the furious woman, he would not venture to interfere directly, but sought to soften her, and said beseechingly, "Don't beat the boy quite to pieces, or he won't be able to look for the lost cow. We shall get more profit out of him if you don't quite kill him."

"True enough," said the woman, "his carrion won't be worth as much as the good beef." Then she gave him a few more good whacks, and packed him off to look for the cow, saying, "If you come back without the cow, I'll beat you to death."

The boy ran from the door sobbing and crying, and went back to the forest where he had been with the herd in the daytime, and searched all night, but could not find a trace of the cow anywhere. But when the sun rose next morning, he made up his mind what to do.

"Whatever may happen to me," he said, "I won't go back again."

Then he made a start, and ran straight forward at one stretch, till he had left the house far behind him. He himself could not tell how far he ran before his strength failed, and he sank down half dead when it was already almost noon. When at length he awoke from a long heavy sleep, he felt something cool in his mouth, and on opening his eyes, he saw a little old man with a long grey beard putting the ladle back into a milk-can.

"Please give me a little more to drink," said the boy. "

You have had enough for today," answered the old man. "If I had not been passing this way by accident, you would have slept your last sleep, for you were already half dead when I found you."

Then the old man asked the boy where he came from and where he was going. The boy related everything that had happened to him, as far back as he could remember, down to last night's beating. The old man listened attentively to the story, but without interrupting, and after a while he remarked, "My dear child, you have fared neither better nor worse than many others whose dear friends and protectors lie beneath the sod. As you have run away, you must seek your fortune elsewhere in the world. But as I have neither house nor farm, nor wife nor child, I cannot do anything to help you but give you good advice gratis. Sleep here quietly through the night, and tomorrow morning note carefully the exact spot where the sun rises. You must proceed in that direction, so that the sun shines in your face every morning, and on your back every evening. Every day you will feel stronger, and after seven years you will see a great mountain before you, so high that its summit reaches to the clouds. There you will find your future fortune.

"Take my wallet and my flask, and you will find as much food and drink in them as you require each day. But take care always to leave a crumb of bread and a drop of liquid untouched, or else your store of food will fail you. You may give freely to a hungry bird or to a thirsty animal, for God is pleased when one of His creatures is kind to another. You will find a folded plantain-leaf at the bottom of the wallet, which you must take the greatest care of. When you come to a river or lake on your journey, spread the leaf on the water, and it will immediately change into a boat which will carry you over to the other side. Then fold the leaf together again, and put it into your wallet."

After thus speaking, he gave the wallet and the flask to the boy, and said, "God bless you!" The next moment he had vanished from the boy's eyes.

The boy would have supposed it to be all a dream, if he had not held the wallet and flask in his hand to convince him that it was a reality. He then looked into the wallet, where he found half a loaf, a small case of salt herrings, another of butter, and a nice piece of bacon. When the boy had eaten enough, he lay down to sleep, with the wallet and flask under his head, so that no thief should be able to take them from him. Next morning at sunrise he awoke, refreshed himself with food and drink, and then set out on his journey.

It was strange that he felt no weariness, and only hunger made him aware that it was nearly noon. He ate the good fare with relish, took a nap, and travelled on. He found that he had taken the right course when the sun set behind his back. He travelled for many days in the same direction, when he arrived on the bank of a small lake. Now he had an opportunity of testing the properties of the leaf. All happened as the old man had foretold, for a small boat with oars lay before him on the water. He stepped in, and a few good strokes of the oars landed him on the other side. Then the boat changed back into a leaf, and he put it into his wallet.

Thus the boy travelled for several years, without the provisions in his flask and wallet failing. Seven years may well have passed, for he had now become a strong youth, when one day he beheld afar off a lofty mountain which seemed to reach the clouds. But a whole week passed before he could reach its foot. Then he sat down to rest, and to see whether the predictions of the old man would be accomplished.

He had not sat there very long when a strange hissing fell upon his ear, and immediately afterwards an enormous serpent appeared, at least twelve fathoms long, which came quite close to the young man. Horror seized him, and he was unable to move, but the serpent passed by him in a moment. Then all was still awhile, but afterwards it seemed to him as if something heavy was moving along in sudden leaps. This proved to be a great toad, as large as a foal of two years old. This ugly creature also passed by without taking any notice of the youth. Then he heard a rushing noise above him, as if a great storm had arisen, and when he looked up, he saw a great eagle flying over his head in the direction which the serpent and the toad had taken.

"These are queer things to bring me good fortune," thought the youth.

Suddenly he beheld a man on a black horse riding towards him. The horse seemed to have wings to his feet, for he flew like the wind. When the man saw the youth sitting at the foot of the mountain, he reined in his horse and asked, "Who has passed by here?"

The youth answered, "First of all a great serpent, perhaps twelve fathoms long, then a toad as large as a two-year-old foal, and lastly a great eagle high above my head. I could not guess at his size, but the sound of his wings was like that of a tempest."

"You have seen well," answered the stranger. "These are my worst enemies, and I am now in pursuit of them. I might take you into my service, if you have nothing better in view. Climb over the mountain, and you will come straight to my house. I shall be there as soon as you, if not sooner."

The young man promised to come, and the stranger rode away like the wind.

The youth did not find it easy to climb the mountain. It was three days before he could reach the summit, and three days more before he reached the foot of the mountain on the opposite side. His new acquaintance was standing in front of his house, and he informed him that he had succeeded in killing the serpent and the toad, but that he had not been able to reach the eagle. Then he asked the young man if he was willing to engage himself as his servant. "You can have as much good food as you want every day, and I will give you liberal wages too, if you will do your duty faithfully."

The bargain was struck, and the master took his new servant into the house, and showed him what he had to do. A cellar was hewn in the rock, and closed with threefold doors of iron. "My savage dogs are chained in this cellar," said the master, "and you must take care that they do not dig their way out under the door with their paws. Know that if one of these savage dogs got loose, it would no longer be possible to restrain the others, for each would follow the other and destroy everything which lives upon the earth. If the last dog should break out, the end of the world would come, and the sun would have shone for the last time." Then he led his servant to a hill which was not created by God, but heaped together by human hands from immense blocks of stone.

"These stones," said the master, "have been heaped together so that a fresh stone can always be rolled up as often as the dogs dig out a hole. I will show you the oxen which drag the stones, in the stall, and instruct you about everything else which you have to attend to."

In the stall were a hundred black oxen, each of which had seven horns, and they were fully as large as the largest oxen of the Ukraine. "Six yoke of oxen harnessed before the waggon will drag a stone easily away. I will give you a crowbar, and when you touch the stone with it, it will roll into the waggon of itself. You see that your work is not very laborious, but your vigilance must be great in proportion. You must look to the door three times during the day, and once at night, in case any misfortune should happen, for the mischief might be much greater than you would be able to answer for to me."

Our friend soon comprehended his duties, and his new occupation was just to his taste. Each day he had the best of everything to eat and drink that a man could wish for. After two or three months the dogs had scratched a hole under the door large enough to put their tails out, but a stone was immediately rolled against the breach, and the dogs were forced to begin their work afresh.

Many years passed by, and the young man had accumulated a good store of money. Then the desire awoke in him to mingle with other men again, for it was so long since he had seen any human face except his master's. Although his master was kind, the young man found the time terribly long, especially when his master took the fancy to have a long sleep. At such times he slept for seven weeks at a stretch, without interruption, and without showing himself.

It chanced that the master had fallen into one of his deep slumbers, when one day a great eagle descended on the hill of stones and began to speak. "Are you not a great fool to sacrifice your pleasant life to good living? The money which you have saved is quite useless to you, for there are no men here who require it. Take your master's swift horse from the stable, bind your bag of money to his neck, leap on his back, and ride away in the direction in which the sun sets, and after some weeks you will again find yourself among men. But you must bind the horse fast with an iron chain, so that he cannot run away, or he would return to his usual haunts, and your master would come to fight with you. But if he is without the horse, he cannot leave the place."

"But who will watch the dogs here, if I go away while my master sleeps?" asked the young man.

"A fool you are, and a fool you will remain," replied the eagle. "Are you not yet aware that God has created him for the express purpose of guarding the hell-hounds? It is from sheer laziness that he sleeps for seven weeks at a stretch. When he has no stranger as a servant, he will be obliged to rouse himself and do his own work himself."

This advice delighted the young man. He followed the counsel of the eagle, took the horse, bound the bag of gold on his neck, leaped on his back, and rode away. He had not ridden very far from the mountain when he heard his master calling after him, "Stop, stop! Take your money and begone in God's name, but leave me my horse!" The youth paid no heed, but rode away, and after some weeks he found himself once more among mortal men. Then he built himself a nice house, married a young wife, and lived happily as a rich man. If he is not dead, he must be still living, but the wind-swift horse died long ago.

Dog Tails – Canine Fairy Tales, Myths And Legends

The Old Dog

A Cossack Tale

This story has been edited and adapted from Robert Nisbet Bain's Cossack Fairy Tales and Folk Tales, first published in 1916 by George G. Harrap & Company, London.

There was once a man who had a dog. While the dog was young he was made much of, but when he grew old he was driven out of doors. So he went and lay outside the fence, and a wolf came up to him and said, "Doggy, why so down in the mouth?"

"While I was young," said the dog, "they made much of me, but now that I am old they beat me."

The wolf said, "I see your master in the field; go after him, and perchance he'll give you something."

"Nay," said the dog, "they won't even let me walk about the fields now, they only beat me."

"Look now," said the wolf, "I'm sorry, and will make things better for you. Your mistress, I see, has put her child down beneath that wagon. I'll seize it, and make off with it. Run after me and bark, and though you have no teeth left, tousle me as much as you can, so that your mistress may see it."

So the wolf seized the child, and ran away with it, and the dog ran after him, and began to tousle him. His mistress saw it, and made after them with a harrow, crying at the same time, "Husband,

husband, the wolf has got the child! Gabriel, Gabriel, don't you see? The wolf has got the child!"

Then the man chased the wolf, and got back the child. "Brave old dog!" said he; "you are old and toothless, and yet you can give help in time of need, and will not let your master's child be stolen."

And henceforth the woman and her husband gave the old dog a large lump of bread every day.

The Owl And Lamp, And The Dogs And The Ragman

A Spanish Tale

This piece is a re-telling of an original poem from Tomás de Iriarte's book Literary Fables of Yriarte, published by Ticknor and Fields in London in 1855. The book is a significant collection of fables by the Spanish writer and poet Tomás de Iriarte.

There are a group of vile critics, cowardly knaves, who wait to attack authors until their victims are, alas, safely quiet in their graves. They know living men might answer back.

To this point, my old grandmother once sang me a little song about a wandering owl that one day found her way into a convent - no, it must have been night, as owls do not fly by day.

Without a doubt, the sun had long since set below the horizon. As she flew along, the owl encountered a lamp or lantern in a passage. I'm unsure which it was.

Turning back reluctantly and angrily, she spoke her mind: "Ah, lamp! How I would love to suck the oil out of you tonight, but your bright light blinds me! If I find you unlit some other night, I'll be ready to feast, I swear."

Denounced as I may be by cowardly critics whom I expose here, for I dare to reveal their meanness, they shall see their portrait in another fable before I close.

A ragman was beating an old dustpan when two dogs, barking furiously like Cerberus, eyed him curiously. As vagabond men do, they howled savagely.

A tall greyhound told them, "Leave the wretch alone. He is someone who strips the reeking skin off dead dogs to sell for bread. You can't win any honour by attacking him. I'll bet this conscious rogue will run from living dogs."

The Ass And The Little Dog

A French Tale

This tale is my own version of a traditional French folk tale.

One's inherent talent cannot be diverted from its natural course through force. Trying to mimic the refined manners of city folk often only results in a poor imitation for country bumpkins. Our Maker grants the gift of charm to only a select few. It is wiser for the rest of us to accept this truth, unlike a certain foolish donkey in a fable. This donkey believed he could win his master's favour by jumping on him and acting affectionately.

In his heart, the donkey questioned why it was the dog's privilege to live a comfortable life in the company of his master and mistress, while he endured the pain of the whip. What did the dog do to deserve affection? Merely offering his paw seemed enough. The donkey decided he could do the same thing, and perhaps even better.

With this idea in mind, the donkey approached his master, who was leisurely seated outdoors. With clumsy movements, he lifted his bruised and battered hoof and attempted to mimic the dog's gesture. He awkwardly patted his master's chin and let out what he believed to be a friendly bray.

But instead of receiving praise, the donkey's actions provoked his master's anger. His master called for a club, and Martin obediently brought one. The poor donkey received a beating, and thus ended the ill-fated comedy.

The Story Of The Partridge, The Fox And The Hound

A Romanian Tale

This story has been adapted from an anonymous original translated by Moses Gaster that appeared in Rumanian Bird and Beast Stories, published in 1915 by Sidgwick & Jackson, Ltd., London.

Once upon a time there was a partridge, and that partridge was sorely troubled, for no one in this world is safe from trouble and worry. Her trouble was that for some time back she was not able to rear her young, because of Auntie Fox, who made a royal feast of the young brood. No sooner did the fox find out that the partridge had hatched her young, than she tied some brambles to her tail, and, dragging it along the ground, pretended to plough the land, close to the place where the partridge had her nest. Turning to the partridge, the fox would say, "How dare you trespass on my land. Off you go, in case I eat you up."

The partridge, frightened, would run away, and the fox would eat the young. This had gone on for three years. On the fourth year it so happened that, while the partridge was weeping, just as a man will do out of worry and grief, she met a hound.

"What is the matter with you, friend, why do you weep so, what ails you, why are you so inconsolable?"

"Oh!" said the poor bird, "I am full of trouble."

Then the hound said sympathetically, "What has happened to you?"

"What has happened to me? Oh, dear friend, so many years have I tried to rear my young, and no sooner do I see God's blessing when Auntie Fox, with the brambles and thorns trailing behind her tail, comes and claims the land, and says, 'Have you again hatched young on my land? Get you off in case I eat you.' And I am so frightened that I run away, and the fox then takes the family and leaves me childless."

The bird stopped here and looked despairingly at the hound. She wondered what he could do for her. But no one knows where help may come from, and just when it is least expected it comes. And so it happened to the bird. The dog who had been sitting all the time, listening as it were with half-closed ears, suddenly shook himself and said, "Is that the trouble which ails you?"

"Yes, that is my trouble."

"Well, if that be so, let me come with you, and maybe I shall be of some help."

And so they both went to the partridge's nest. There the dog crouched behind the bushes and waited for the fox to come. He had not to wait very long until the fox came with the brambles tied to her tail, and, pulling it along, made pretence of ploughing the land, saying, "Now then you partridge, are you trespassing again…"

But the fox was not allowed to finish the sentence, for out of the bushes sprang the dog. The fox took to her legs, running as fast as they would carry her. Now, whether the hound ran or did not run I do not know, but I certainly can say that the fox ran for all she was worth and raised a cloud of dust behind her. And so she ran and ran until she reached her lair, and she buried herself deep in the ground, very thankful to have saved her skin from the jaws of death. The hound, wearied, tired, and vexed that the fox had escaped, settled down at the mouth of the lair waiting for the chance that the fox would come out again, so that he might set his eyes upon her, but it was all in vain, for the fox, once safe, never dreamt of coming out again. But then the fox, having nothing else to do, started talking to herself.

"Clever fox, clever fox, I know that you take care of your skin. Well, you did well to save yourself, and to get safely away from that hound. Now let me ask my eyes, 'What did you do when the hound was after me?'"

"Well, we, turning right and left, looked out to see which way we could save you and hide you."

"Dear eyes," said the fox, and full of satisfaction, she stroked them with her paws.

"Now I will ask my forelegs."

"And you, my forelegs, what did you do when the hound was chasing me?"

"What did we do? We ran as fast as we could to carry you safe to the lair and to save you."

"Very good, then, my darlings," and she kissed them and stroked them lovingly.

Then she asked the hind legs.

"What did you do when the hound was chasing me?"

"What did we do? We raised the dust and threw it into his eyes to save you."

"My darlings," again the fox said, and licked them and caressed them, "so must you always do."

The fox, having nothing else to do, said, "I must now ask you, tail, 'What did you do, Oh my tail?'"

"I, what was I to do? I waddled to the right and left and yet he never caught me. If it were not for the legs, I am afraid I should not see the sun anymore, and neither would you, Oh fox."

"As you say, then, you are the only one who did not help me, you are my enemy, for if it were not for the blessed legs, none of us would have seen the sun anymore. All right, out you go, you fool. you must no longer be with me or with my darling eyes."

And, turning round, she crawled backwards and pushed it out of the lair. The hound, who was sitting outside, was just waiting for this, and no sooner did he see the bush of the tail coming out than he pounced on it and, getting hold of it, he pulled with all his might and dragged out tail and fox together. And that was the end of the fox. The fox may have been very clever, but the old proverb is true: "Each animal dies through his own tongue." And since that time the partridge hatches her young unmolested, and the land of the fox has remained unploughed.

Dog Tails – Canine Fairy Tales, Myths And Legends

The Lame Dog

A Swedish Tale

This story has been adapted from an original by Clara Stroebe that appeared in The Swedish Fairy Book, published in 1921 by Frederick A. Stokes Company, New York.

Once upon a time there lived a king, like many others. He had three daughters, who were young and beautiful to such a degree that it would have been difficult to have found handsomer maidens. Yet there was a great difference among them, for the two older sisters were haughty in their thoughts and manners, while the youngest was sweet and friendly, and everyone liked her. Besides, she was as fair as the day and as delicate as the snow, and far more beautiful than either of her sisters.

One day the king's daughters were sitting together in their room, and their talk happened to turn on their husbands-to-be. The oldest said, "If I ever marry, my husband must have golden hair and a golden beard!"

And the second exclaimed: "And mine must have silver hair and a silver beard!"

But the youngest princess held her tongue and said nothing. Then her sisters asked her whether she did not want to wish for a husband. "No," she answered, "but if fate should give me a husband, I will be content to take him as he is, and were he no more than a lame dog."

Then the two other princesses laughed and joked about it, and told her the day might easily come when she would change her mind. But many speak truth and do not know it!

Thus it chanced with the king's daughters, since before the year had come to an end, each had the suitor for whom she had wished. A man with golden hair and golden beard sued for the oldest princess and won her consent to his suit. And a man with silver hair and a silver beard sued for the second and she became his bride, but the youngest princess had no other suitor than a lame dog.

Then she recalled her talk with her sisters in their room, and thought to herself: "May God aid me in the marriage into which I must enter!" Yet she would not break the word she had once passed, but followed her sisters' example and accepted the dog. The wedding lasted a number of days and was celebrated with great pomp and splendour. But while the guests danced and amused themselves, the youngest princess sat apart and wept, and when the others were laughing, her tears flowed till it made one sad to see them.

After the wedding the newly married pairs were each to drive off to their castle. And the two older princesses each drove off in a splendidly decorated coach, with a large retinue, and all sorts of honours. But the youngest had to go afoot, since her husband, the dog, had neither coach nor driver. When they had wandered long and far, they came to a great forest, so great that it seemed endless, but the dog limped along in advance, and the king's daughter followed after, weeping. And as they went along she suddenly saw a magnificent castle lying before them, and round about it were beautiful meadows and green woods, all of them most enjoyable to see. The princess stopped and asked to whom the great mansion might belong.

"That," said the dog, "is our home. We will live here, and you shall rule it as you see fit."

Then the maiden laughed amid her tears, and could not overcome her surprise at all she saw. The dog added: "I have but a single request to make to you, and that you must not refuse to grant."

"What is your request?" asked the princess.

"You must promise me," said the dog, "that you will never look at me while I am asleep, otherwise you are free to do whatever you wish."

The princess gladly promised to grant his request, and so they went to the great castle. And if the castle was magnificent from without, it was still more magnificent within. It was so full of gold and silver that the precious metals gleamed from every corner, and there was such abundance of supplies of every kind, and of so many other things, that everything in the world one might have wished to have was already there. The princess spent the live-long day running from one room to another, and each was handsomer than the one she had just entered. But when evening came and she went to bed, the dog crept into his own, and then she noticed that he was not a dog, but a human being. Yet she said not a word, because she remembered her promise, and did not wish to cross her husband's will.

Thus some time passed. The princess dwelt in the beautiful castle, and had everything her heart might desire. But every day the dog ran off, and did not reappear until it was evening and the sun had set. Then he returned home, and was always so kind and friendly that it would have been a fine thing had other men done half as well. The princess now began to feel a great affection for him, and quite forgot he was only a lame dog, for the proverb says: "Love is blind."

Yet time passed slowly because she was so much alone, and she often thought of visiting her sisters and seeing how they were. She spoke of it to her husband, and begged his permission to make the journey. No sooner had the dog heard her wish than he at once granted it, and even accompanied her some distance, in order to show her the way out of the wood.

When the king's daughters were once reunited, they were naturally very happy, and there were a great many questions asked about matters old and new. And marriage was also discussed. The oldest princess said, "It was silly of me to wish for a husband with golden hair and golden beard; for mine is worse than the meanest troll, and I have not known a happy day since we married."

And the second went on, "Yes, and I am no better off, for although I have a husband with silver hair and a silver beard, he dislikes me so heartily that he begrudges me a single hour of happiness."

Then her sisters turned to the youngest princess and asked how she fared. "Well," was her answer, "I really cannot complain, for though I only got a lame dog, he is such a dear good fellow and so kind to me that it would be hard to find a better husband."

The other princesses were much surprised to hear this, and did not stop prying and questioning, and their sister answered all their questions faithfully. When they heard how splendidly she lived in the great castle, they grew jealous because she was so much better off than they were. And they insisted on knowing whether there was not some little thing of which she could complain. "No," said the king's daughter, "I can only praise my husband for his kindness and amiability, and there is but one thing lacking to make me perfectly happy."

"What is it?" "What is it?" cried both sisters with a single voice.

"Every night, when he comes home," said the princess, "he turns into a human being, and I am sorry that I can never see what he really looks like."

Then both sisters again with one voice, began to scold the dog loudly, because he had a secret which he kept from his wife. And since her sisters now continually spoke about it, her own curiosity awoke once more, she forgot her husband's command, and asked how she might manage to see him without his knowing it.

"Oh," said the oldest princess, "nothing easier! Here is a little lamp, which you must hide carefully. Then you need only get up at night when he is asleep, and light the lamp in order to see him in his true shape."

This advice seemed good to the king's daughter; she took the lamp, hid it in her breast, and promised to do all that her sisters had counselled.

When the time came for them to part, the youngest princess went back to her beautiful castle. The day passed like every other day. When evening came at last and the dog had gone to bed, the princess was so driven by curiosity that she could hardly wait until he had fallen asleep. Then she rose, softly, lit her lamp, and drew near the bed to look at him while he slept. But no one can describe her astonishment when throwing the light on the bed, she saw no lame dog lying there, but the handsomest youth her eyes had ever beheld. She could not stop looking at him, but sat up all night bending over his pillow, and the more she looked at him the handsomer he seemed to grow, until she forgot everything else in the world. At last the morning came. And as the first star began to pale in the dawn, the youth began to grow restless and awaken. The princess much frightened, blew out her lamp and lay down in her bed. The youth thought she was sleeping and did not wish to wake her, so he rose quietly, assumed his other shape, went away and did not appear again all day long.

And when evening came and it grew late, everything happened as before. The dog came home from the forest and was very tired. But no sooner had he fallen asleep than the princess rose carefully, lit her lamp and came over to look at him. And when she cast the light on his bed it seemed to her as though the youth had grown even handsomer than the day before, and the longer she looked the more handsome he became, until she had to laugh and weep from sheer love and longing. She could not take her eyes from him, and sat all night long bent over his pillow, forgetful of her promise and all else, only to be able to look at him. With the first ray of dawn the youth began to stir and awake. Then the princess was again frightened, quickly blew out her lamp and lay down in her bed. The youth thought she was sleeping, and not wishing to waken her, rose softly, assumed his other shape, went away and was gone for the entire day.

At length it grew late again, evening came and the dog returned home from the forest as usual. But again the princess could not control her curiosity. No sooner was her husband sleeping than she rose quietly, lit her lamp, and drew near carefully in order to look at him while he slept. And when the light fell on the youth, he appeared to be handsomer than ever before, and the longer she looked the more handsome he grew, until her heart burned in her breast, and she forgot all else in the world looking at him. She could not take her eyes from him, and sat up all night bending over his pillow. And when morning came and the sun rose, the youth began to move and awaken. Then the princess was much frightened, because she had paid no heed to the passing of time, and she tried to put out her lamp quickly. But her hand trembled, and a warm drop of oil fell on the youth and he awoke. When he saw what she had done, he leaped up, terrified, instantly turned into a lame dog, and limped out into the forest. But the princess felt so remorseful that she nearly lost her senses, and she ran after him, wringing her hands and weeping bitterly, and begging him to return. But he did not come back.

The king's daughter now wandered over hill and dale, along many a road new to her, in order to find her husband, and her tears flowed the while till it would have moved a stone. But the dog was gone and stayed gone, though she looked for him North and South. When she saw that she could not find him, she thought she would return to her handsome castle. But there she was just as unfortunate. The castle was nowhere to be seen, and wherever she went she was surrounded by a forest black as coal. Then she came to the conclusion that the whole world had abandoned her, sat down on a stone, wept bitterly, and thought how much rather she would die than live without her husband.

At that a little toad hopped out from under the stone, and said, "Lovely maiden, why do you sit here and weep?"

And the princess answered, "It is my hard fate to weep and never be happy again. First of all I have lost the love of my heart, and now I can no longer find my way back to the castle. So I must perish of hunger here, or else be devoured by wild beasts."

"Oh," said the toad, "if that is all that troubles you, I can help you! If you will promise to be my dearest friend, I will show you the way."

But that the princess did not want to do. She replied: "Ask of me what you will, save that alone. I have never loved anyone more than my lame dog, and so long as I live will never love anyone else better." With that she rose, wept bitterly, and continued her way. But the toad looked after her in a friendly manner, laughed to himself, and once more crept under his stone.

After the king's daughter had wandered on for a long, long way, and still saw nothing but forest and wilderness, she grew very tired. She once more sat down on a stone, rested her chin on her hand, and prayed for death, since it was no longer possible for her to live with her husband. Suddenly there was a rustling in the bushes, and she saw a big grey wolf coming directly toward her. She was much frightened, since her one thought was that the wolf intended to devour her. But the wolf stopped, wagged his tail, and said, "Proud maiden, why do you sit here and weep so bitterly?"

The princess answered, "It is my hard fate to weep and never be happy again. First of all I have lost my heart's dearest, and now I cannot find my way back to the castle and must perish of hunger, or be devoured by wild beasts."

"Oh," said the wolf, "if that is all that troubles you, I can help you! Let me be your best friend and I will show you the way."

But that did not suit the princess, and she replied, "Ask of me what you will, save that alone. I have never loved anyone more than my lame dog, and so long as I live I will never love anyone else better." With that she rose, weeping bitterly, and continued on her way. But the wolf looked after her in a friendly manner, laughed to himself and ran off hastily.

After the princess had once more wandered for a long time in the wilderness, she was again so wearied and exhausted that she could not go on. She sat down on a stone, wrung her hands, and wished for death, since she could no longer live with her husband. At that moment she heard a hollow roaring that made the earth tremble, and a monstrous big lion appeared and came directly toward her. Now she was much frightened; for what else could she think but that the lion would tear her to pieces? But the beast was so weighed down with heavy iron chains that he could scarcely drag himself along, and the chains clashed at either side when he moved. When the lion finally reached the princess he stopped, wagged his tail, and asked, "Beautiful maiden, why do you sit here and weep so bitterly?"

The princess answered, "It is my hard fate to weep and never be happy again. First of all I have lost my heart's dearest, and now I cannot find my way to the castle, and must perish of hunger, or be devoured by wild beasts."

"Oh," said the lion, "if that is all that troubles you, I can help you! If you will loosen my chains and make me your best friend, I will show you the way."

But the princess was so terrified that she could not answer the lion, far less venture to draw near him. Then she heard a clear voice sounding from the forest. It was a little nightingale, who sat among the branches and sang, "Maiden, maiden, loosen his chains!"

Then she felt sorry for the lion, grew braver, went up to him, unloosed his chains and said, "Your chains I can loosen for you, but I can never be your best friend. For I have never loved anyone more than my lame dog and will never love anyone else better."

And then a wondrous thing took place. At the very moment the last chain fell from him, the lion turned into a handsome young prince, and when the princess looked at him more closely, it was none other than her heart's dearest, who before had been a dog. She sank to the ground, clasped his knees, and begged him not to leave her again. But the prince raised her with deep affection, took her in his arms and said, "No, now we shall never more be parted, for I am released from my enchantment, and have proved your faith toward me in every way."

Then there was joy indescribable. And the prince took his young wife home to the beautiful castle, and there he became king and she was his queen. And if they have not died they are living there to this very day.

The Three Dogs

A Swedish Tale (Westergötland)

Gunnar Olof Hyltén-Cavallius was a prominent Swedish folklorist and historian known for his efforts in collecting and preserving Swedish folk tales. One of the stories he collected, titled "The Three Dogs," is featured in George Stephens' book, "Swedish Folk Tales and Adventures. First Part," published in 1844 by A. Bohlin's Publisher in Stockholm. This version is my own translation from a Swedish copy of Stephens' book.

Once upon a time there was a king who went away and married a fair queen. After they had been married for some time, the queen fell into labour and gave birth to one daughter. Then there was great joy over both city and country, because everyone indulged the king well, for the sake of his gentleness and justice. But when the child was born, there entered an old woman, who had a strange appearance, and no one knew where she came from or where she went. The old woman prophesied about the king's child, and said that the child would perish if ever she went under open skies, before she had lived through fifteen winters, for in doing so she would be stolen away by a mountain troll. When the king heard this, he committed the woman's words to memory, and appointed guards who would make sure that the young princess never walked come under the open sky.

Sometime after that, the queen was pregnant again, and gave birth to another daughter. Then there was new joy over the whole kingdom, but the old fortune-teller appeared as before, and warned the king not to let the princess walk under open skies before she turned fifteen winters. While the first two daughters grew, the queen gave birth to her third daughter. Again the old woman came and prophesied that the king's third daughter must suffer the same fate as her older siblings. Then the king became very ill at ease, for he loved his children above all else in the world. He therefore gave strict orders that the three princesses always had to be kept under cover.

Things went well for a while, and the king's children grew up to be the most beautiful and tender-hearted young women, known for their sweet natures far and wide. Then a great war erupted at the borders of his in the land, so that the king their father went away. One day, while he was at war, the three princesses sat by the window, and looked out and saw how the sun shone on the small flowers in the örta farm. They felt a strong urge to play with the beautiful flowers, and asked their guardians for leave to wander around the garden for a little while. The guards would not agree to this, for they were afraid of the king's wrath, but the king's daughters begged them so beautifully that the men could not resist, and let them have their way. The princesses were now very happy, and so went out the garden. But their fun did not last long, for they had hardly skipped out into the open air when until suddenly a cloud descended, which stole them away, and all attempts to find them again were in vain, even though the palace folk searched in all directions.

There was now great sadness and wailing over the whole kingdom, and one can well imagine that the king was not very happy when he came home, and asked how such a tragedy had occurred. But, as the saying goes: 'A deed done has no turning back'. The king had no choice but to accept his family's fate. With no other advice being available, the king issued a command over his entire kingdom, that whoever could save his three daughters from the mountain troll's violence, would get one of them as a wife, and with her half the kingdom. When this was proclamation spread across the neighbouring countries, many friends went out to look for the three princesses.

At the king's court were two foreign princes, who likewise went away in search of the princesses, to try their luck in the quest.. They armed themselves with the best armour and the costliest weapons, and said loudly that they would not return, without having succeeded in this enterprise.

The King's older sons searched everywhere for a long time, looking in every direction. Meanwhile, there was a poor widow who lived deep in the wild forest. She had an only son who would go out daily to play with his mother's boars. One day, while the boy was wandering around, he made himself a pipe and started to play it. He played so beautifully that anyone who heard it felt deeply satisfied. Besides his musical talent, the boy was tall, strong, and free-spirited, and he was not easily frightened by anything.

One day, the shepherd boy was sitting in the forest playing his pipe while his three boars were rooting around under the fir trees. An old, old man came walking by, with a beard so long and wide that it reached far below his belt. The old man had with him a very large and strong dog. When the boy saw the big dog, he thought to himself, "It would be great to have such a dog for company here in the wilderness, for then I wouldn't need anything else!"

Noticing the boy's interest, the old man said, "That's why I came here. I want to exchange my dog for one of your boars."

The boy readily agreed and made the trade, giving the old man his grey boar in exchange for the big dog.

As the old man went on his way, he said, "I think you will be satisfied with our trade because this dog is not like other dogs. His name is Håll, and whatever you ask him to hold, he will hold it, even if it is the fiercest troll."

After saying this, they parted ways, and the boy felt fortunate, believing that luck was on his side that day.

As evening approached, the boy called his dog and drove the boars home from the woods. When his mother learned that he had traded the grey boar for a dog, she became extremely angry and began hitting him with blows and punches. The boy tried to calm her, but it was no use. The longer she raged, the angrier she became.

Seeing that nothing else would work, the boy called his dog and commanded, "Hold!" Immediately, the dog ran forward, caught the old woman, and held her so she couldn't move. However, the dog did not harm her in any other way. The woman had to promise her son that she would accept what had happened, and they made peace with each other. Still, the old woman felt she had suffered a great loss by giving up the fat boar.

On the second day, the boy went to the forest with his dog and both boars. When he arrived, he sat down and played his pipe as usual, and the dog danced so strangely that it was a great wonder to watch. As he sat there, the old, grey-bearded man came walking out of the forest again, this time with another dog, which was no smaller than the first. When the boy saw the beautiful animal, he thought to himself, "It would be great to have another dog for company here in the wilderness. Then I wouldn't need anything else!"

Noticing the boy's interest, the old man said, "That's why I came here. I want to exchange my dog for one of your boars."

The boy hesitated for a moment but eventually agreed to the trade. He got the big dog and gave the old man his boar. As the grey-bearded man departed, he said, "I think you'll be satisfied with our deal, because this dog is not like other dogs. His name is Slit, and whatever you ask him to tear apart, he will rip it to pieces, even if it's the fiercest troll."

After parting ways, the boy was pleased with the trade, even though he knew his mother would not be happy.

When it got late and the boy returned home, the old woman was just as upset as the day before. However, she didn't dare to hit her son this time, fearing his large dogs. Eventually, as often happens, she calmed down and they reconciled. Still, the old woman felt she had suffered a significant loss.

On the third day, the boy went to the forest again, this time with his remaining boar and his two dogs. Feeling happy, he sat down on a stump and played his pipe, while the dogs danced amusingly. As he sat in peace, the old, grey-bearded man appeared once more, now with a third dog, just as large as the others. When the boy saw the beautiful animal, he couldn't help but think, "It would be great to have that dog for company here in the wilderness. Then I really wouldn't need anything else!"

The old man spoke up, "That's why I came here. I want to sell you my dog because I can see that you would like to own him."

The boy immediately agreed and made the trade, giving his last boar for the dog. As the old man departed, he said, "I think you'll be satisfied with our bargain because this dog is not like other dogs. His name is Ly, and he has such fine hearing that he perceives everything from miles away. He even hears the trees growing and the grass sprouting from the ground."

After their conversation, they parted on friendly terms, for the boy was very happy with his new dogs, feeling that now he had nothing to fear in the world.

As evening approached and the boy returned home, his mother became very sad that her son had sold all their boars. However, the boy reassured her, promising that she wouldn't suffer any lack. His words cheered her up, and she thought he spoke both wisely and confidently.

When dawn broke, the boy went hunting with his dogs. Each night, he returned home with as much game as he could carry. He continued hunting like this for some time, until his mother's home was abundantly supplied with food and other necessities. Then, he bid his mother a fond farewell, took his dogs, and said he wanted to venture out into the world to seek his fortune.

The boy travelled over mountains and through wild paths, eventually arriving deep in a dark forest. There, he met the old greybeard again. The boy was very happy and greeted him, saying, "Good day, father! Thanks for the last time we met."

The old man replied, "Good day again! Where are you headed?"

The boy explained, "I'm going out into the world to see what fortune has in store for me."

The old man said, "Keep going straight, and you will come to the king's court, where your fortune awaits."

After that, they parted ways. The boy followed the greybeard's advice and continued on without rest. Wherever he stopped at an inn, he played his pipe and let his dogs dance, always receiving food and provisions in return.

After traveling for a long time, the boy finally arrived at a large city, where many people were gathered in the streets. Curious about the commotion, he made his way to where the king's edict was being announced: whoever could save the three princesses from the mountain trolls would win one of them in marriage, as well as half the kingdom. The boy realized this was what the greybeard had hinted at. He called his dogs and made his way to the king's court.

At the royal court, there was only wailing and sorrow ever since the day the king's daughters disappeared, with the king and queen mourning the most. The boy went up to the castle and offered to play for the king and show his dogs' tricks. This pleased the courtiers, as they thought it might lift their master's spirits. The boy was admitted and given an audience.

When the king heard the boy's music and saw the strange dancing of the dogs, he was delighted. He hadn't been so happy in seven long years, ever since the day he lost his daughters.

After the dance was over, the king asked the boy what reward he wanted for bringing such great joy to everyone. The boy replied, "Lord King, I have not come here to seek goods and gold. Instead, I have another request: to be given permission to seek out and rescue the three princesses who are in the grip of the mountain trolls."

When the king heard this, his heart grew heavy, and he said, "You must not think it will be easy to save my daughters. This is a difficult task, and many better than you have failed. But if someone does save the princesses, I will not break my word."

The boy found this to be a manly and royal promise. He then took leave of the king and set out on his journey, determined not to rest until he found what he was looking for.

The boy travelled through many large countries without encountering anything unusual. His dogs followed him faithfully. Ly always ran ahead and alerted him if anything was sensed nearby, Hold carried the food sack, and Slit, the strongest, carried the boy when he grew tired.

One day, Ly came running quickly to his master and reported that he had been by a high mountain and heard the king's daughter spinning inside, and the giant himself was not home. The boy was very happy and hurried to the mountain with his dogs. When they arrived, Ly said, "We have no time to waste. The giant is only ten miles away, and I can already hear the golden shoes of his horse clinking against the stones."

The boy commanded his dogs to break down the mountain door, which they did. Inside, he saw a fair maiden sitting in the mountain hall, twisting gold thread on a gold spindle. The boy greeted her kindly. The princess was amazed and said, "Who are you, who dares to come here into the giant's hall? In the seven long years I've been here, I have never seen a human being. For God's sake, hurry out before the troll comes home, or your life will be in danger."

But the boy was not afraid and decided to wait for the giant's arrival. While they were still talking, the giant came riding on his golden-shod steed. Seeing the door open, he became very angry and roared so loudly that the whole mountain shook. "Who has broken my mountain door?" he bellowed.

The boy answered boldly, "I did, and now I want to break you too. Hold! Hold him; Slit and Ly! Tear him into a thousand pieces."

As soon as the words were spoken, the dogs rushed forward, attacked the giant, and tore him into countless pieces. The princess was overjoyed and exclaimed, "God be praised! Now I am saved." She then embraced the boy and kissed him. But the boy did not want to stay any longer. He saddled the giant's steed, loaded it with all the goods and gold in the mountain, and quickly left with the beautiful princess.

They travelled a long way together, and the boy treated the princess with respect and courtesy, as a noble maiden should be courted. One day, Ly, who had run ahead to scout, came rushing back to his master, saying that he had been to a high mountain and heard the second king's daughter inside, spinning gold yarn. The giant was not home. The boy was pleased with this news and hurried to the mountain, with his faithful dogs following him.

When they arrived, Ly said, "We have no time to waste. The giant is only eight miles away, and I can already hear the gold shoes of his horse clinking against the stones."

The boy ordered his dogs to break down the mountain door, which they did. Inside, he saw a fair maiden sitting in the mountain hall, spinning gold yarn on a golden spindle. He greeted her warmly. The princess was surprised and said, "Who are you, who dares to come here in the giant's hall? In the seven years I've been here, I have never seen a human being." She added, "For God's sake, leave before the troll returns, or it will cost you your life."

But the boy told her his purpose and resolved to face the giant. While they were still talking, the giant arrived on his gold-shod horse and stopped outside the mountain. Seeing the door open, he became furious and roared so loudly that the mountain trembled. "Who has broken my mountain door?" he bellowed.

The boy answered boldly, "I did, and now I will break you too. Hold! Hold him; Slit and Ly! Tear him into a thousand pieces."

The dogs immediately rushed forward, attacked the giant, and tore him into as many pieces as leaves falling in autumn.

The princess was overjoyed and exclaimed, "God be praised! Now I am saved." She then embraced the boy and kissed him. The boy brought the princess to her sister, and there was great joy when they were reunited. He then gathered all the goods in the mountain hall, loaded them onto the giant's gold-shod horse, and set off with the two princesses.

They travelled a long way together again, and the boy served the princesses with honour and respect, as noble maidens deserved. One day, Ly, who had run ahead to scout, came rushing back and said that he had been to another high mountain and heard the third king's daughter inside, weaving gold cloth. The giant was not home. The boy was pleased with this news and hurried to the mountain, with his three dogs following him.

When they arrived, Ly said, "We have no time to waste. The giant is only five miles away. I can hear the golden shoes of his horse clinking against the stones."

The boy ordered his dogs to break down the mountain door, which they did. Inside, he saw a maiden weaving on a gold loom. She was exceedingly beautiful, and the boy thought he had never seen such a fair woman in his life. He greeted her warmly. The princess was greatly astonished and said, "Who are you, who dares to come here in the giant's hall? In the seven years I've been here, I have never seen a human being." She added, "For God's sake, leave before the troll returns, or it will cost you your life."

But the boy was in high spirits and said he would gladly risk his life for the beautiful princess.

While they were still talking, the giant came riding on his golden-shod horse and stopped under the mountain. When he entered and saw the uninvited guests, he was horrified, knowing well what fate had befallen his brothers. He thought it best to resort to trickery and cunning, as he did not dare to engage in an open fight. The giant then began to speak pleasantly and acted smooth and friendly towards the boy and his dogs. At the same time, he commanded the king's daughter to cook, pretending to be hospitable. The boy, fooled by the giant's smooth talk, let his guard down and sat down at the table with him. The king's daughter cried, and the dogs were troubled, but no one paid attention to them.

After the meal, the boy said, "I have now satisfied my hunger, give me something to quench my thirst!"

The giant replied, "There is a spring up in the mountain that flows with the clearest wine, but I have no one to fetch it."

The boy said, "If that's the case, one of my dogs can go up there." The giant smiled in his false heart, for he wished the boy would send his dogs away. The boy ordered Håll to go to the well for wine, and the giant handed him a large pot. The dog went reluctantly, and he didn't return.

After a while, the giant said, "I wonder why the dog is taking so long. Maybe you should send your other dog to help him, as the way is long and the pot is heavy."

Not suspecting any betrayal, the boy agreed and sent Slit to find out why Håll hadn't returned. The dog wagged its tail and was reluctant to leave, but the boy didn't notice and sent him away. The giant smiled slyly, and the king's daughter cried, but the boy paid no attention and remained cheerful, joking with his host.

A long time passed, but neither wine nor dogs were heard from. The giant said, "It seems your animals don't obey you; otherwise, we wouldn't still be sitting here thirsty. It's best you send Ly to find out what's happened."

The boy, urged by the giant's words, ordered his third dog, Ly, to go to the spring. Ly, however, whined and crawled at his master's feet, but the boy angrily drove him away. The dog obeyed reluctantly and ran up the mountain. When he arrived, he found the others trapped by a high wall, imprisoned by the giant's sorcery.

With all three dogs captured, the giant rose, changed his demeanour, and grabbed a shiny sword from the wall. He said, "Now I will avenge my brothers, and you will soon die, for you are in my power."

The boy was horrified and regretted sending away his dogs. He said, "I don't beg for my life, for I must die someday. But I beg to read my Pater Noster and play a hymn on my pipe. This is the custom in my country."

The giant consented but warned he would not wait long. The boy knelt, devoutly read a Pater Noster, and began to play his pipe, so that it echoed over the mountains and valleys. In that moment, the sorcery lost its power, and the dogs were freed. They came rushing like a storm wind into the mountain hall. The boy stood up and shouted, "Hold! hold him; Slit and Ly! tear him to pieces."

The dogs fell upon the giant and tore him into countless pieces. The boy then took all the goods in the mountain, harnessed the giant's horses to a gilded frame, and left as quickly as he could.

When the king's daughters met again, there was great joy, as one can imagine, and everyone thanked the boy for saving them from the mountain trolls. The boy fell in love with the youngest princess, and they pledged their faith and honour to each other. They continued their journey with play, jokes, and all kinds of joy, and the boy served them with respect and honour, as courtly maidens deserved. During the journey, the princesses played with the boy's hair and each tied a golden ring to his long curls as a keepsake.

One day, while they were still on the road, they met two wandering men traveling the same route. The strangers were in worn clothes, their feet were wounded, and it was clear they had made a long journey. The boy asked them who they were and where they came from. The strangers replied that they were two princes searching for the three princesses taken by the mountain trolls, but their journey had been unsuccessful, and they were now returning home more like beggars than princes. Hearing this, the boy felt compassion for the two wanderers and invited them to join him in his fine carriage. The princes were very grateful for this kindness. They travelled together and entered the kingdom where the king, the princesses' father, ruled.

When the princes learned how the boy had saved the three princesses, they became envious, feeling their own journey had been fruitless. They conspired to betray the boy and claim the honour and tribute for themselves. They hid their evil intentions until they found a suitable opportunity. Then, they suddenly pounced on the boy, seized him by the neck, and threatened the princesses with death if they did not swear to conceal what had happened. The princesses, being in the power of the princes, dared not refuse this request. They felt great pity for the boy who had risked his life for them, and the youngest princess mourned him deeply, refusing to enjoy any joy.

After committing this great betrayal, the princes went to the king's court. It was a joyous occasion as the king was reunited with his three daughters. Meanwhile, the poor boy lay in the forest, as if dead. However, he was not entirely abandoned, as his faithful dogs lay around him, warming his body against the cold and licking his wounds. They did not leave until their master stirred and came back to life.

After regaining his health and strength, he began to journey forward again and eventually reached the king's court where the princesses resided. When the boy arrived, he noticed great merriment and jokes throughout the yard, and from the king's hall, he heard dances and beautiful string music. He was greatly astonished and asked what all the celebration was about.

A servant replied, "Surely you must have come from a long way, not to know that the king has recovered his daughters from the mountain trolls. Today is the wedding of the two oldest princesses."

The boy then inquired about the youngest princess, whether she too was a bride. The servant answered that she did not want any man but only cried, and no one knew the cause of her great sorrow. The boy was happy again, realizing that his fiancée remained devoted and faithful to him.

The boy then went up to the castle and asked the king if he could add to the wedding festivities by showing his dogs. The king was pleased with this request and commanded that the stranger be received warmly. When the boy entered the hall, there was great amazement among the entire wedding crowd at his impressive appearance and demeanour. It seemed to everyone that such a bold and fine young man was a rare sight. The three princesses immediately recognized him and sprang up from the table, rushing into his arms. The princes, seeing this, did not wish to stay long where they were.

The princesses told how the boy had saved them and recounted all that had happened. They pointed out the gold rings tied in his hair curls as proof. When the king realized that the two foreign princes had betrayed the boy, he became very angry and ordered them to be driven away from the royal court.

The brave boy, however, was honoured greatly for his deeds, as he deserved. That same day, he married the youngest princess. After the king's death, the boy was crowned lord of the land and became a just and happy king. He ruled happily with his fair queen, and they live happily to this day. And with that, I wasn't there anymore.

Dog And His False Friend Leopard

An African Tale

This story has been edited and adapted from Robert Hamill Nassau's Where Animals Talk, first published in 1912 by Richard G. Badger at The Gorham Press, based out of Boston. This tale was originally told by storytellers from the Benga tribe.

Dog and Leopard built a town. Dog then had very many children. Leopard had many children too. They had one table together. They conversed, they hunted, they ate, they drank.

One day, they were arguing. Leopard said, "If I hide myself, you are not able to see me."

Dog replied, "There is no place in which you can hide where I cannot see you."

The next day, at the break of the day, Leopard emerged from his house at Batanga, and he went north as far as from there to Bahabane near the Plantation. Dog, woke up later that morning and asked, "Where is chum Njâ?"

The women and children answered, "We do not know."

Dog decided to find his friend, and as he went, smelling the scent of Leopard, he soon arrived at the Plantation. He came and stood under the tree up which Leopard was hidden and he said, "There you are!"

Both of them returned, and came to their town. Food had been prepared, and they ate. Leopard said, "Chum, you will not see me here tomorrow."

When the next day began to break, Leopard started southward, as far as Lolabe. Later that morning Dog stood out in the street, lifted up his nose, and smelled. He also went down southward, clear on till he came to Lolabe, and standing at the foot of a tree, he said, "There you are!"

Leopard came down from the top of the tree. They stood and then they returned to their town. Food was cooked for them; they ate, and finished.

Leopard said, "Chum, you will not see me tomorrow again, no matter what may take place."

Dog asked, "Truely?"

Leopard replied, "Yes!"

In the morning, Leopard went southward, for a distance like from Batanga to Campo River, which is about 40 miles.

At the opening of the next day, Dog emerged, and, standing and smelling, he said, looking toward the south, "He went this way." Dog also went to Campo. He reached Leopard, and said, "There you are!"

They came back to their town, where they were made food, and they ate.

The next day, Leopard emerged early. He went northward, as far as from Batanga to Lokonje, again about 40 miles. Dog sniffed the air, and followed him north too. At a steady pace, he was soon there, and he reached Leopard. So, Leopard said, "It is useless, I will not attempt to hide myself again from Mbwa."

Thereupon, Dog spoke to Leopard and said, "It is I, whom, if I hide myself from you, you will not see."

Leopard replied, "What? Even if you were able to find me, how much more should I be able to find you!"

So, Dog said to him, "Wait, till daybreak."

When the next day broke, Dog rushed from his house like a flash unseen, to Leopard's house. Dog lay down underneath Leopard's bed. Then Leopard, who had not seen him, went to Dog's house. He asked the women, "Where is Mbwa?"

They said, "Your friend, long ago, has gone out, very early."

Leopard returned to his house, and he said to his children, "That fellow! If I catch him I do not know what I shall do to him!"

He started southward on his journey, as far as Lolabe, and did not see Dog. So he returned northward a few miles, as far as Boje, and did not see him. Down again south to Campo, and he did not see him. That first day, he did not find him at all. Then he returned toward Batanga, and went eastward to Nkâmakâk, which is about 60 miles, and he did not see him. He went on northward to Ebaluwa, but again he did not see him. He went north-west to Lokonje but he did not see him. And Leopard, wearied, went back to his town.

Coming to the bed, not knowing Dog was still there, he lay down very tired. He said to his people, "If I had met him today, then you would be eating good meat now." All these words were said while Dog was underneath the bed.

Then Dog leaped out, and a surprised Leopard asked, "Where have you been?"

Dog answered, "I saw you when you first went out."

Leopard said, "True?"

And Dog said, "Yes!"

Then Dog went out to his end of the town. And, knowing that Leopard intended evil toward him, he said to his children, "Let us go and dig a pit." So they went and dug a pit in the middle of the road.

Then Dog told his wives and children, "Go away from here at once!" He also said, "I and this little Mbwa, which can run so fast, we shall remain behind." Then the others went on in advance.

Dog warned this young one, "When you are pursued, you must jump clear across that pit."

Then Dog, to cover the retreat of his family, came alone to Leopard's end of the town. Leopard and his children chased after him. Dog ran away rapidly, and escaped.

When Leopard's company arrived at Dog's house, all they found there was that little dog. So they said, "Come on, for there is no other choice than we catch and eat this little thing."

Thereupon, Leopard chased after the little dog, but it leaped away rapidly, and Leopard ran after him. When the little Dog was near the pit, it made a jump. When Leopard came to the pit, he fell inside, tumbling! Dog's other enemy Gorilla was following after Leopard. He also fell into the pit, headlong! Finding Leopard there, Gorilla said, "What is this?"

Leopard stood at one side, and Gorilla at the other. They paced around and around each other snarling and cursing.

Dog, standing at the edge above, was laughing at them, saying, "Fight your own fight! Wasn't it me that you wanted? "

But Leopard and Gorilla were not fighting in the pit. If one approached, the other retreated.

Dog spoke to them and said in derision. "I am just a weakling, but I have outwitted both of you!"

The Dog Gellert

A Welsh Tale

This story has been edited and adapted from Sabine Baring-Gould's Curious Myths of the Middle Ages, first published in 1867 by Roberts Brothers, Boston. This tale is a variation of the Gellert legend that I published in the book, Tales From The Land Of Dragons.

The Welsh Prince Llewellyn had a noble deerhound, Gellert, whom he trusted to watch the cradle of his baby son whilst he was absent.

One day, on his return, to his intense horror, he beheld the cradle empty and upset, the clothes dabbled with blood, and Gellert's mouth dripping with gore. Llewellyn concluded hastily that the hound had proved unfaithful and had fallen on the child and devoured it. In a paroxysm of rage the prince drew his sword and slew the dog.

I the very next moment the cry of the babe from behind the cradle showed him that the child was uninjured; and, on looking farther, Llewellyn discovered the body of a huge wolf, which had entered the house to seize and devour the child, but which had been kept off and killed by the brave dog Gellert.

In his self-reproach and grief, the prince erected a stately monument to Gellert, and called the place where he was buried after the poor hound's name.

Cerberus

A Greek Tale

This tale is my own version of a traditional Greek myth.

In the depths of the underworld, guarded by shadows and surrounded by flames, stood the gates of Hades. Beyond these gates lay the realm of the dead, ruled by the fearsome god of the underworld himself. But even Hades needed protection, and so he employed the fiercest guardian known to mortals and gods alike: Cerberus, the three-headed hound.

Cerberus was no ordinary dog. Each of his heads was as large as a boulder, with eyes that glowed like embers in the darkness. His fur was black as midnight, and his teeth were sharper than any blade. With three pairs of eyes, Cerberus watched over the gates of the underworld, ensuring that no soul escaped its grasp.

Legend had it that Cerberus was born from the blood of the monstrous Titans, the ancient enemies of the gods. When Zeus, the king of the gods, waged war against the Titans, Cerberus emerged from the depths of Tartarus, the darkest pit of the underworld, ready to do battle.

But instead of fighting against the gods, Cerberus pledged his loyalty to Hades, the ruler of the underworld. In return, Hades granted Cerberus the task of guarding the gates of the underworld for all eternity.

For centuries, Cerberus faithfully carried out his duty, allowing only the souls of the dead to pass through the gates of Hades. His fearsome appearance struck terror into the hearts of mortals and gods alike, and none dared to challenge his authority.

But despite his ferocity, Cerberus had a softer side. Legend had it that he was fond of a few select beings, including Persephone, the queen of the underworld, and Orpheus, the legendary musician who dared to descend into the realm of the dead in search of his beloved.

Though Cerberus remained a formidable guardian, his loyalty to Hades never wavered. He stood watch over the gates of the underworld, a silent sentinel in the darkness, ready to defend his master's realm against any who dared to trespass.

And so, the legend of Cerberus endured, a testament to the power of loyalty, duty, and the unyielding strength of the underworld.

Mr. Fox's Housewarming

An American Tale

This story has been edited and adapted from Abbie Phillips Walker's book, Sandman's Goodnight Stories first published in 1921 by Harper & Brothers.

Mr. Fox had been so much disturbed by Mr. Dog and his master that he decided to try living somewhere besides on the ground floor of the woods.

One night he took a look around in the moonlight, and to his delight he discovered the very place for him to live.

It was a house built in the branches of a big tree that some boys very likely had made the year before. "Now with a very little repairing this will be the finest house in the woods," said Mr. Fox.

So over the hill he ran to Mr. Man's and brought away all that was needed to make his house comfortable.

He even found an old piece of stovepipe to make his stove draw well, and in a few days Mr. Fox told all his friends of his new home and invited them to a housewarming.

Mr. Coon and Mr. Possum and Mr. Squirrel were not at all upset by finding out that Mr. Fox's new home was in the big tree, but Mr. Rabbit and Mr. Badger looked very sad and said it was out of the question for them to accept Mr. Fox's kind invitation, much as they would like to come.

Mr. Fox had borrowed a ladder from Mr. Man, and when Mr. Rabbit and Mr. Badger said they could not come Mr. Fox remembered that he was not much of a climber himself and that if he did not keep that ladder he might have a hard time getting into his home when he was in a hurry.

So he decided that Mr. Man would not need it as much as he would and that it would also make a nice addition to his home.

When he told Mr. Badger and Mr. Rabbit about the ladder they decided to come, and one night when the moon was shining the animals were all to go to Mr. Fox's house to dinner.

Mr. Fox thought it would be the cheapest way to fill his guests with soup, so he took all the bones that he had collected and put them in a pot on the stove to boil.

Up curled the smoke from his chimney and out through the windows went the nice-smelling odour of soup, and Mr. Dog, who happened to be running through the woods, saw and smelled as well.

He wagged his tail and looked up at the house in the tree. Then he whined and scratched the tree, and as he danced about it, with his eyes fixed upon the house all the time, he bumped into the ladder.

"Ah, how fortunate!" he said, and up he went and into Mr. Fox's house he went, too, and took the cover off the pot.

It did not take him a second to remove the pot from the stove and pour out the soup in the sink and cool those bones, and then he had such a feast.

He ate until he became sleepy, then he lay down on the floor and went to sleep.

Mr. Dog did not dream that Mr. Fox lived in that house, not that he was afraid of him, but he would have slept with one eye open so that he could catch him if he had known.

Mr. Fox was out roaming over the hill, looking about for a stray turkey or hen, and he did not come home until it was nearly dark.

He ran up the ladder, and without striking a light he went toward the stove to see how his soup was getting on, and stumbled over Mr. Dog. Up jumped Mr. Dog with a gruff bark, and Mr. Fox, not stopping for the ladder, jumped out of the window and almost broke his neck, while Mr. Dog looked after him, barking and yelping in a terrible manner.

Mr. Fox did not stop. He kept on running, and Mr. Dog, thinking of the bones he did not finish, turned away from the window and began to eat. While he was eating the guests for the housewarming began to arrive. Mr. Coon did not need the ladder to help him, or Mr. Possum, either, nor did Mr. Squirrel, but as it was there they felt it would not be polite to enter any other way.

Mr. Possum started up first, and behind him Mr. Coon. Then came Mr. Badger, and Mr. Rabbit behind him, while Mr. Squirrel ran up the side of the ladder.

When they were about halfway up, Mr. Dog, hearing a noise outside, went to the door, and of all the surprised creatures you ever saw, the guests were the most surprised, unless it was Mr. Dog. He forgot to bark for a second, he was so taken back.

Then he recovered and out of the door he went, but he was not used to going down a ladder, and on the first rung he slipped and down he went.

The guests started to jump just as Mr. Dog barked, but they were not out of the way when Mr. Dog fell, and down they all tumbled, Mr. Dog, Mr. Possum, Mr. Coon and Mr. Badger.

Mr. Squirrel jumped, too, but he jumped for a limb of the tree and was not in the mix-up. He said it was the funniest sight he ever saw, and he had a fine view from where he sat.

But Mr. Rabbit said he was sure his view of the affair was the best, for, being nearest the bottom of the ladder when the tumble began, he was up and out of the way when they all came down on the ground.

"You could not tell who was who or which from the other," said Mr. Rabbit, later talking it over with Mr. Squirrel.

It was a long time before Mr. Fox could make the guests believe he had not planned to have Mr. Dog at his house-warming, but when Mr. Squirrel told them that he had seen the bones on the floor and the kettle in the sink they finally forgave Mr. Fox.

He decided the ground floor was the safest for him, after all, and when he was once again settled he gave a feast, and this time Mr. Dog was not there.

Ned Dog And Billy Goat

An American Settler Tale

This story has been edited and adapted from Sarah Johnson Cocke's Bypaths in Dixie, first published in 1911 by E. P. Dutton and Company, New York.

One day Mister Man went out to hunt a dog and a goat for his little boy. He saw Sister Dog and her family on the side of the road, and they seemed to be in a mighty commotion about something. Mister Man yelled and asked what was wrong. Sister Dog said she found one of Sister Nanny Goat's kids laying out in the pasture just bleating all by itself, and she didn't know what to do with it. Mister Man said, "I'll take care of it, and I'd like mightily to take care of one of your kids, too."

Sister Dog told him "certainly," that it would make her terribly proud for one of her kids to live up at his fine house. So Mister Man lifted the goat and the puppy up onto Miss Racehorse's back alongside him and flew across the country to his house.

When Mister Man's wife saw him, she threw up her hands and said, "Lord, Mister Man, what do you expect to do with that goat?"

Mister Man said, "Oh! I'll just put it out here with the puppy and raise them both together."

Mister Man's boy felt glad. They put a pan of milk out in the cow house, and both of the creatures ate out of it together. When they got big enough to eat like real animals, the little boy put out goat feed for the goat and dog food for the dog.

The dog was just named Collie Dog when he lived with his mommy, but when he started living with people, the little boy named him Ned.

The goat, of course, was named Billy. When Billy Goat looked at his feed, and Ned Dog looked at his food, they both felt mighty proud, except they couldn't understand why it wasn't mixed together. So Billy ran over and tried to eat bones and meat, and Ned ran to Billy's box and tried to eat hay and bran mash. They kept on trying to eat each other's food as long as they lived. Eventually, Billy grew so big that he started grazing around amongst the flowers and grass, because the flower buds tasted nicer to him than grass. So Mister Man's old lady started arguing and insisting that he tether the goat.

Well, when Billy found himself tied to that rope so he couldn't go in the house or in the flower garden, he just cried and cried. Ned Dog tried to stay with him as much as he could, but when he saw Mister Man and the little boy setting off down the road on Miss Racehorse and her little colt, his feet just naturally started moving without him realizing it. His heart told him to go back and stay with Billy, but his feet said they weren't going to do any such thing. Of course, he couldn't help himself if his feet refused to take him home. After a while, when he got back, Billy was crying himself sick. He said he didn't understand why he was tied up and Ned Dog wasn't, and Ned Dog said he didn't either, because you see, Ned thought Billy was a dog, and Billy thought he was a dog too. That's the way with some folks. Many of them think they're big dogs when they're nothing but old goats!

Mister Man's son wanted to untie Billy, but he dare not touch the tether because his mother would be angry of he did. Around about dinner time, Ned got so miserable listening to Billy howling that he started gnawing and pulling at the stake. Then he tried to scratch it up, but it was too deep. So he started pulling at the rope again, and eventually, the knot came undone. He caught the knot in his teeth and then told Billy to go wherever he pleased. Billy kicked up his legs and flew down the road with Ned Dog behind him, holding onto the rope. Billy ate all along the road, and Ned Dog followed wherever Billy chose to go, because Ned felt the responsibility of freeing Billy. After a while, Ned Dog begged Billy to come home! He told him his jaws were nearly broken from clamping onto that knot. But Billy said he wasn't going until he had eaten his fill of those flower buds. Billy wasn't thinking about Ned as long as he could enjoy himself. Ned started to howl and bark with the jaw ache, but Billy was too full of himself to notice Ned.

Billy kept going, and Ned was just dragging along with the jaw ache until eventually, they came to the old log fence around the pasture. Billy tried to jump the fence, but Ned crawled through, but you see, Billy couldn't jump high enough because Ned was pulling the rope on the other side, so Billy got tangled up on one of the rails. Ned ran back when he saw Billy hanging, but he got back through a different hole again, and that twisted the rope so tight that Billy got in a mighty bad fix before you knew it. He started bleating and yelling, and Ned dropped the rope and started to howl, but that never did any good, and it never does any good in this world.

Realising that there was no good to come of howling, Ned leaped out and ran home, and he barked at Mister Man and ran out towards the road. He barked at the little boy and ran out again, but none of them could understand why he was acting so strange. He ran out into the backyard and howled and barked, and the little colt asked him what was wrong, he told him Billy was almost choked to death, hanging on the pasture fence. The colt gave a jump over the back fence, and he and Ned took off, tearing down the big road. The little boy and Mister Man saw the colt break loose, and they flew after him, and all of them got to Billy just in time to keep him from choking to death."

The truth is that Billy never quite had enough rope to kill himself with on that fence, but if he had had a little more rope, him and all the other foolish folks like him would have been dead long ago!

The Origin Of The Dog

A South American Tale From the peoples of the Andes

This tale is my own version of a traditional South American myth.

In ancient times, humans lived in harmony with the natural world, and animals and humans could communicate with each other. However, as humans began to build villages and cultivate crops, they became increasingly reliant on domesticated animals for labour and companionship.

One day, a group of humans encountered a pack of wild wolves while hunting in the mountains. The humans admired the wolves' strength, agility, and loyalty to their pack and wished to have similar companions for themselves. They prayed to the spirits of the mountains, asking for guidance on how to tame the wild wolves.

In response to their prayers, the spirits of the mountains transformed one of the fiercest and most loyal wolves into the first domesticated dog. This dog became known as the *guardian of humanity* and served as a faithful companion and protector to humans.

Over time, the descendants of this first domesticated dog spread throughout the world, forming close bonds with humans and playing crucial roles in their lives as herders, hunters, guardians, and companions.

This legend reflects the deep connection between humans and dogs in South American cultures and highlights the importance of dogs as valued members of society. It also underscores the reverence and respect that indigenous peoples hold for the natural world and the spiritual beliefs that shape their relationships with animals.

Dog And Repo

A Finnish Tale

This tale is adapted from Eero Salmelainen's book, Fairy Tales And Stories Of The Finnish People, published by the Finnish Literary Society in 1852.

Shepherds were tending their cattle, and their dog was with them. A fox (referred to as "repo" in Finnish) kept running with the dog, but the dog was timid and didn't dare to attack the repo.

The shepherds meanwhile wished that the dog would kill the repo to protect their livestock. They followed this advice. They cut off a piece of the dog's tail and sent the children back to the cattle with the dog.

The repo did not appear that day and there was no sport between dog and fox. The children returned home at the end of the day. Their parents asked, "Did the repo run with the dog again?"

The children replied, "It didn't happen."

The parents then said, "Go again tomorrow, for it will come then."

The children did as they were told, and soon the repo appeared. The repo and the dog started running and competing with each other again until, finally, the repo caught the dog by the tail. In great pain, the dog got angry and killed the repo, and so the fox was lost.

Where The Sparks Go

An American Tale

This story has been edited and adapted from Abbie Phillips Walker's book, The Sandman's Hour first published in 1917 by Harper & Brothers.

One night when the wind was blowing and it was clear and cold out of doors, a cat and a dog, who were very good friends, sat dozing before a fire-place. The wood was snapping and crackling, making the sparks fly. Some flew up the chimney, others settled into coals in the bed of the fireplace, while others flew out on the hearth and slowly closed their eyes and went to sleep.

One spark ventured farther out upon the hearth and fell very near Pussy. This made her jump, which awakened the dog.

"That almost scorched your fur coat, Miss Pussy," said the dog.

"No, indeed," answered the cat. "I am far too quick to be caught by those silly sparks."

"Why do you call them silly?" asked the dog. "I think them very good to look at, and they help to keep us warm."

"Yes, that is all true," said the cat, "but those that fly up the chimney on a night like this certainly are silly, when they could be warm and comfortable inside. For my part, I cannot see why they fly up the chimney."

The spark that flew so near Pussy was still winking, and she blazed up a little when she heard the remark the cat made.

"If you knew our reason you would not call us silly," she said. "You cannot see what we do, but if you were to look up the chimney and see what happens if we are fortunate enough to get out at the top, you would not call us silly."

The dog and cat were very curious to know what happened, but the spark told them to look and see for themselves. Pussy was very cautious and told the dog to look first, so he stepped boldly up to the fireplace and thrust his head in. He quickly withdrew it, for his hair was singed, which made him cry and run to the other side of the room.

Miss Pussy smoothed her soft coat and was very glad she had been so wise. She walked over to the dog and urged him to come nearer the fire, but he realized why a burnt child dreads the fire, and remained at a safe distance.

Pussy walked back to the spark and continued to question it. "We cannot go into the fire," she said. "Now, pretty, bright spark, do tell us what becomes of you when you fly up the chimney. I am sure you only become soot and that cannot make you long to get to the top."

"Oh, you are very wrong," said the spark. "We are far from being black when we fly up the chimney, for once we reach the top, we live forever sparkling in the sky. You can see, if you look up the chimney, all of our brothers and sisters, who have been lucky and reached the top, winking at us almost every night. Sometimes the wind blows them away, I suppose, for there are nights when we cannot see the sparks shine."

"Who told you all that?" said the cat. "Did any of the sparks ever come back and tell you they could live forever?"

"Oh no!" said the spark; "but we can see them, can we not? And, of course, we all want to shine forever."

"I said you were silly," said the cat, "and now I know it. Those are not sparks you see, they are stars in the sky."

"You can call them anything you like," replied the spark, "but we make the bright light you see."

"Well, if you take my advice," said the cat, "you will stay right in the fireplace, for once you reach the top of the chimney out of sight you go. The stars you see twinkling are far above the chimney, and you never could reach them."

But the spark would not be convinced. Just then someone opened a door and the draught blew the spark back into the fireplace. In a few minutes it was flying with the others toward the top of the chimney.

Pussy watched the fire a minute and then looked at the dog.

"The spark may be right, after all," said the dog. "Let's go out and see if we can see it."

Pussy stretched herself and blinked. "Perhaps it is true," she replied. "Anyway, I will go with you and look."

Black Shuck

An English Tale from East Anglia

This tale is my own version of a traditional English legend that probably has its roots in old Saxon and Norse storytelling.

On a stormy night in the remote countryside of East Anglia, a small we fly to a village nestled amidst the rolling hills. The villagers whispered tales of an ancient curse that plagued their land, a curse embodied by a monstrous creature known as Black Shuck.

Black Shuck was no ordinary dog. With fur as dark as midnight and eyes that glowed with an otherworldly light, it was said to roam the moors and marshes, preying on unsuspecting travellers who dared to venture out after dark.

Among the villagers was a young woman named Emily. She had heard the stories of Black Shuck since childhood, but she dismissed them as mere superstition, believing herself to be immune to the fears that gripped her neighbours.

One fateful evening, as the wind howled and the rain lashed against the windows, Emily's curiosity got the better of her. Determined to disprove the existence of Black Shuck once and for all, she set out into the night, armed with nothing but a lantern and her own bravery.

As Emily wandered deeper into the darkness, she felt a sense of unease creeping over her. The shadows seemed to shift and twist, and the air was heavy with the scent of damp earth and decay.

Suddenly, she heard the sound of heavy footsteps behind her, followed by a low growl that sent shivers down her spine. Emily's heart pounded in her chest as she turned to face the source of the noise, her lantern trembling in her hand.

There, emerging from the darkness, was Black Shuck. The creature loomed before her, its eyes burning like smouldering coals, and Emily felt a wave of terror wash over her.

Paralyzed with fear, she stood rooted to the spot as Black Shuck advanced, its jaws dripping with saliva and its claws scraping against the ground. Emily knew she had to run, but her legs refused to obey her commands.

With a guttural snarl, Black Shuck lunged forward, its massive form blotting out the moonlight as it closed in on its prey. Emily closed her eyes and braced herself for the inevitable, her screams echoing through the night.

But just as Black Shuck was about to strike, a sudden flash of lightning illuminated the scene, revealing the creature's true form. To Emily's horror, she saw not a monstrous dog, but a twisted amalgamation of flesh and bone, its eyes empty sockets and its mouth a gaping maw of razor-sharp teeth.

With a bloodcurdling howl, Black Shuck vanished into the darkness, leaving Emily trembling and alone in the night. She stumbled back to the village, her mind reeling with the horrors she had witnessed, and vowed never to venture out after dark again.

From that day forth, the legend of Black Shuck lived on in the village, a terrifying reminder of the dangers that lurked in the shadows. And though Emily survived her encounter with the creature, she knew that some horrors were too terrible to be forgotten.

Dog And The Kingship

An African Tale

This tale has been edited and adapted from Kate Douglas Wiggin and Nora Archibald Smith's collection, The Talking Beasts, A Book of Fable and Wisdom, and illustrated by Harold Nelson. The book was published in 1922.

Some people wanted to invest Mister Dog with the honour of their kingship. They sought out all the things of royalty, the cap, the sceptre, the rings, and the skin of mulkaka.

When everything was ready they said, "The day has come to install Mister Dog as our king."

The headmen all came in their full number and regalia. They sent for the players of drum and marimba. They spread coarse mats and fine mats. Where the lord was going to sit, they laid down a coarse mat. They then spread a fine mat on top of that. They set a chair on top of the fine mat.

They said, "Let the lord sit down."

He sat down. The people served the celebratory food and drink. He, Mister Dog, on seeing the breast of a fowl, felt the pangs of great greed grasp him. He stood up in haste, took the breast of the fowl, and ran into the bush.

The people said, "The lord, whom we are crowning today, has run away with the breast of the fowl into the bush!"

The people packed everything away and went home. Mister Dog lost his chance to be their king because he was, at heart, a thief.

I have told my little tale and I am finished.

The Youth And The Dog-Dance

A First Nations Tale From Canada

This tale has been edited and adapted from Cyrus Macmillan's collection, Canadian Fairy Tales. The book was published in 1922 by John Lane at The Bodley Head.

Once long ago, when the People dwelt in the country in the north-west, a youth went far away from his native village to catch birds. His people lived near a lake where only small birds nested, and as he wanted large and bright-coloured feathers for his arrows and his bonnet he had to go far into the forest, where larger birds of brilliant plumage lived. When he reached the Land of Many Feathers far in the north country, he dug a pit on the top of a high hill. Then he covered the pit with poles and over the poles he spread grass and leaves so that the place looked like the earth around it. He put meat and corn on the grass, and tied the food to the poles so that the birds could not carry it away. Then he climbed down into the pit and waited for the birds to come, when he could reach up and catch them by the feet and kill them.

All day long and far into the night the youth waited for birds, but no birds came. Towards morning he heard a distant sound like that of a partridge drumming. But the sound did not come nearer. The next night, as the youth watched and waited in the pit, he heard the same sound, and he said, "I will see where the noise comes from and I will discover the cause, for it is not a partridge, and it is very strange."

So he climbed out of the pit and went in the direction of the sound. He walked along rapidly through the forest until he came at dawn to the shore of a large lake. The drumming came from somewhere in the lake, but as he stood listening to it, the sound suddenly stopped.

The next night the youth heard the drumming louder than before. Again he went to the lake. The sound was again distinct as it rose from the water, and when he looked he saw great numbers of birds and animals swimming in the lake in the moonlight. But there was no explanation of the strange sound. As he sat watching the animals and birds, he prayed to his guardian spirit to tell him the cause of the drumming. Soon an old man came along. He was old and bent and wrinkled, but his eyes were kind. The youth gave him some tobacco and they sat down together on the edge of the lake and watched the swimmers in the dim light, and smoked their pipes.

"What are you doing here?" asked the old man.

"I am trying to learn the cause of the strange drumming," said the youth.

"You do well indeed to seek it," said the old man, "and to seek to know the cause of all things. Only in that way will you be great and wise. But remember there are some things the cause of which you can never find."

"Where have you come from?" said the boy.

"Oh," said the man, "I lived once upon a time like you in the Country of Fancy where great Dreams dwell, and indeed I live there still, but your dreams are all of the future while mine are of the past. But some day you too will change and your thoughts will be like mine."

"Tell me the cause of the drumming," said the boy.

And the old man said, "Take this wand that I will give you and wave it before you go to sleep, and maybe you will see strange things."

Then he gave the boy a wand and disappeared into the forest and the boy never saw him again. The boy waved the wand and fell asleep on the sand as the old man had told him. When he awoke he found himself in a large room in the midst of many people. Some of them were dancing gracefully, and some sat around and talked. They wore wonderful robes of skins and feathers, of many different colours. The boy wished he could get such feathers for his own clothes and his bonnet. But as he looked at the people he was suddenly aware that they were none other than the animals and birds he had seen for two nights swimming in the lake in the moonlight. They were now changed into human form, through some strange and miraculous power. They were very kind to the youth and treated him with great courtesy.

At last the dancing ceased and the talking stopped, and one who seemed to be the Chief stood up at the end of the room and said, "Oh, young stranger, the Great Spirit has heard your prayers, and because of your magic wand we have been sent to you in these shapes. The creatures you see here are the animals and birds of the world. I am the Dog, whom the Great Spirit loves well. I have much power, and my power I shall give to you, and I shall always protect you and guard you. And even if you should treat me with cruelty I shall never be unfaithful to you, nor shall I ever be unkind. But you must take this Dance home with you and teach it to your people and they must celebrate the Dance once a year."

Then he taught the youth the secrets of their Dance.

When the youth had learned the Dance, the Chief turned to his companions and said, "My comrades and brothers, I have taught the young stranger the secrets of the Dance. I have given him my own power. Will you not have pity on a creature from earth and give him some of the power of which you too are possessed?"

For a long time no one spoke, but at last Owl arose and said, "I too will help him. I have power to see far in the darkness, and to hunt by night. When he goes out at night I will be near him and he shall see a great distance. I give him these feathers to fasten in his hair."

And the Owl gave him a bunch of feathers, which the youth tied to his head.

Then Buffalo came forward and said, "I too will help him. I will give him my endurance and my strength, and my power to trample my enemies underfoot. And I give him this belt of tanned buffalo-hide to wear when he goes to war."

And he gave the youth a very wondrous belt to fasten around his waist.

The animals and birds, one after the other, gave him gladly of their power. Porcupine gave him quills with which to decorate his leather belt and his bonnet, and he said, "I too will aid you, and when you make war I will be near you. I can make my enemies as weak as children, and they always flee when I approach, for they fear the shooting of my quills. When you meet your foes you will always overcome them, for I give you power as it was given to me."

And Bear said, "I will give you my toughness and my strength, and a strip of fur for your leather belt and your coat. And when you are in danger, I will not be far away."

Then Deer said, "I give you my swiftness so that you may be fleet of foot. And when you pursue your enemies you will always overtake them, and should you flee from them, you will always out-run them in the race."

Then the birds spoke again, and Crane said, "I give you a bone from my wing to make a war-whistle to frighten your enemies away or to summon your people to your assistance when you need them. And I give you my wings for your head-dress."

The giant Eagle then spoke and said, "Oh, youth, I will be with you wherever you go, and I will give you my strength and my power in war. And even as I do, you will always see your enemies from afar, and you can always escape them if you so desire." And he gave him a large bunch of wonderful eagle feathers to tie in his hair as a token of his fidelity.

And finally, Wild-Cat said, "I give you my power to crawl stealthily through the grass and the underbrush and to spring unexpectedly on your foes and take them unawares. And I give you too my power of hiding from my enemies." And he gave him strips of his fur to decorate his clothing in token of his friendship.

From all the animals and the birds the youth received power and gifts. Then he waved his magic wand and lay down to sleep. When he awoke, he found himself on the shore of the lake, and far in the east the dawn was breaking. But he could see farther than he had ever seen before, and away in the distance he could make out blue hills and smoke rising from far-off villages. And he knew that strange power was upon him. But not a sound came from the lake, and the drumming had for ever ended.

The youth took his magic wand and his gifts and set out for his home. And he told his people what had happened and he taught them the secrets of the Dance which was to make them strong and victorious in war. And among his people it became a great ceremony and was practised for long ages, and was known as the Dog-Dance. And since that time, the animals and birds have been friends to the People, and the People have acquired much of their cunning and skill and power. And ever after the night of moonlight by the lake when the youth with the magic wand received the strange gifts, the People have decorated their war clothes with fur and quills and feathers from the animals and the birds. And in the far north country, the Dog-Dance is still held at intervals out of gratitude for the gifts, for the People do not forget the promise of long ago.

The Story Of Kitinda And Her Wise Dog

An African Tale

This tale has been edited and adapted from Henry Morton Stanley's book, My Dark Companions, published in 1893 by Sampson, Lowe, Marston and Company, London.

Kitinda, a woman of the Basoko, near the Aruwimi river, possessed a dog who was remarkable for his intelligence. It was said that he was so clever that strangers understood his motions as well as though he talked to them, and that Kitinda, familiar with his ways and the tones of his whines, his yelps, and his barks, could converse with him as easily as she could with her husband.

One market-day the mistress and her dog agreed to go together, and on the road she told him all she intended to do and say in disposing of her produce in exchange for other articles which she needed in her home. Her dog listened with sympathy, and then, in his own manner, he conveyed to her how great his attachment to her was, and how there never was such a friend as he could be, and he begged her that, if at any time she was in distress, she would tell him, and that he would serve her with all his might. Then he said, "It's only because I am afraid of the effects of being too clever, that I have not served you oftener and much more than I have done."

"What do you mean?" said Kitinda.

"Well, you know, among the Basoko, it is supposed, if one is too clever, or too lucky, or too rich, that it has come about through dealings in witchcraft, and people are burned in consequence. I do not like the idea of being burned, and therefore I have refrained from assisting you because I feared you could not contain your surprise, and would chat about it to the villagers. Then someday, after some really remarkable act of cleverness of mine, people would say, 'Ha! This is not a dog. No dog could have done that! He must be a demon, or a witch in a dog's hide!' and of course they would take me and burn me."

"Why, how very unkind of you to think such things of me! When have I chatted about you? Indeed I have too many things to do, my housework, my planting and marketing so occupy me, that I could not find time to gossip about my dog."

"Well, it is already notorious that I am clever, and I often tremble when strangers look at and admire me for fear some muddle-headed fellow will fancy that he sees something else in me more than unusual intelligence. What would they say, however, if they really knew how very sagacious I am? The reputation that I possess has only come through your affection for me, but I assure you that I dread this excess of affection in case it should end fatally for you and for me."

"But are you so much cleverer than you have already shown yourself? If I promise that I will never speak of you to any person again, will you help me more than you have done, if I am in distress?"

"You are a woman, and you could not prevent yourself talking if you tried ever so hard."

"Now, look here, my dog. I vow to you that no matter what you do that is strange, I wish I may die, and that the first animal I meet may kill me if I speak a word. You shall see now that Kitinda will be as good as her word."

"Very well, I will take you at your word. I am to serve you every time you need help, and if you speak of my services to a soul, you are willing to lose your life by the first animal you may meet."

Thus they made a solemn agreement as they travelled to market.

Kitinda sold her palm-oil and fowls to great advantage that day, and in exchange received sleeping-mats, a couple of carved stools, a bag of cassava flour, two large well-baked and polished crocks, a bunch of ripe bananas, a couple of good plantation hoes, and a big strong basket.

After the marketing was over she collected her purchases together and tried to put them into the basket, but the big crocks and carved stools were a sore trouble to her. She could put the flour and hoes and the bananas on top with the mats for a cover very well, but the stools and the crocks were a great difficulty.

Her dog in the meantime had been absent, and had succeeded in killing a young antelope, and had dragged it near her. He looked around and saw that the market was over, and that the people had returned to their own homes, while his mistress had been anxiously planning how to pack her property.

He heard her complain of her folly in buying such cumbersome and weighty things, and ask herself how she was to reach home with them.

Pitying her in her trouble, the dog galloped away and found a man empty-handed, before whom he fawned and whose hands he licked, and being patted he clung to his cloth with his teeth and pulled him gently along, wagging his tail and looking very amiable. He continued to do this until the man, seeing Kitinda fretting over her difficulty, understood what was wanted, and offered to carry the stools and crocks at each end of his long staff over his shoulders for a few of the ripe bananas and a lodging. His assistance was accepted with pleasure, and Kitinda was thus enabled to reach her home, and on the way was told by the man how it was that he had happened to return to the marketplace.

Kitinda was very much tempted there and then to dilate upon her dog's well-known cleverness, but remembered in time her promise not to boast of him. When, however, she reached the village, and the housewives came out of their houses, burning to hear the news at the market, in her eagerness to tell this one and then the other all that had happened to her, and all that she had seen and heard, she forgot her vow of the morning, and forthwith commenced to relate the last wonderful trick of her dog in dragging a man back to the marketplace to help her when she thought that all her profit in trade would be lost, and when she was just about to smash her nice crocks in her rage.

The dog listened to her narrative, viewed the signs of wonder stealing over the women's faces, heard them call out to their husbands, saw the men advancing eagerly towards them, saw them all look at him narrowly, and then heard one man exclaim, "That cannot be a dog! It is a demon within a dog's hide. He…"

But the dog had heard enough. He turned, and ran into the woods, and was never more seen in that village.

The next market-day came round, and Kitinda took some more palm-oil and a few fowls, and left her home to dispose of them for some other domestic needs. When she had travelled about half-way, her dog came out of the wood, and after accusing her of betraying him to her stupid countrymen, thus returning evil for good, he sprang upon her and tore her to pieces.

Dog Tails – Canine Fairy Tales, Myths And Legends

The Dog Bride

A folk tale from India - Santal

This tale has been edited and adapted from Cecil Henry Bompas' book, Folklore of the Santal Parganas, published in 1909 by The Indian Civil Service.

Once upon a time there was a youth who used to herd buffaloes, and as he watched his animals graze he noticed that exactly at noon each day a she-dog used to make its way to a ravine, in which there were some pools of water. This made him curious and he wondered to whom the dog belonged and what it did in the ravine, so he decided to watch, and one day when the dog came he hid himself and saw that when it got to the water, it shed its dog skin and out stepped a beautiful maiden, and began to bathe, and when she had finished bathing she put on the skin and became a dog again, and went off to the village. The herd boy followed her and watched to see which house she entered, and he enquired to whom the house belonged. Having found out all about it, he went back to his work.

That year the herd boy's father and mother decided that it was time for him to marry and began to look about for a wife for him, but he announced that he had made up his mind to have a dog for his wife and he would never marry a human girl.

Everyone laughed at him for such an extraordinary idea, but he could not be moved. so at last they concluded that he must really have the soul of a dog in him, and that it was best to let him have his own way. So his father and mother asked him whether there was any particular dog he would like to have for his bride, and then he gave the name of the man into whose house he had tracked the dog that he had seen going to the ravine. The master of the dog laughed at the idea that anyone should wish to marry her, and gladly accepted a bride's price for her. so a day was fixed for the wedding and the booth built for the ceremony and the bridegroom's party went to the bride's house and the marriage took place in due form and the bride was escorted to her husband's house.

Every night when her husband was asleep, the bride used to come out of the dog's skin and go out of the house, and when her husband found out this, he one night only pretended to go to sleep and lay watching her, and when she was about to leave the room he jumped up and caught hold of her and seizing the dog skin, threw it into the fire, where it was burnt to ashes. In this way his bride remained a woman, but she was of more than human beauty. This soon became known in the village and everyone congratulated the herd boy on his wisdom in marrying a dog.

Now the herd boy had a friend named Jitu and when Jitu saw what a prize his friend had got, he thought that he could do no better than marry a dog himself. His relations made no objection and a bride was selected and the marriage took place, but when they were putting vermilion on the bride's forehead she began to growl, but in spite of her growling they dragged her to the bridegroom's house, and forcibly anointed her with oil and turmeric, but when the bride's party set off home, the dog broke loose and ran after them. Then everyone shouted to Jitu to run after his bride and bring her back, but she only growled and bit at him, so that he had at last to give it up. Then everyone laughed at him so much that he was too ashamed to speak, and two or three days later he hanged himself.

The Dog And The Corpse

A Russian Tale

This tale has been edited and adapted from Henry Morton Stanley's book, My Dark Companions, published in 1893 by Sampson, Lowe, Marston and Company, London.

A moujik went out in pursuit of game one day, and took a favourite dog with him. He walked and walked through woods and bogs, but got nothing for his pains. At last the darkness of night surprised him. At an uncanny hour he passed by a graveyard, and there, at a place where two roads met, he saw standing a corpse in a white shroud. The moujik was horrified, and did not know which way to go, or whether to keep on or to turn back.

"Well, whatever happens, I'll go on," he thought, and on he went, his dog running at his heels. When the corpse perceived him, it came to meet him, not touching the earth with its feet, but keeping about a foot above it, the shroud fluttering after it. When it had come up with the sportsman, it made a rush at him, but the dog seized hold of it by its bare calves, and began a tussle with it. When the moujik saw his dog and the corpse grappling with each other, he was delighted that things had turned out so well for himself, and he set off running home with all his might. The dog kept up the struggle until cock-crow, when the corpse fell motionless to the ground. Then the dog ran off in pursuit of its master, caught him up just as he reached home, and rushed at him, furiously trying to bite and to rend him. So savage was it, and so persistent, that it was as much as the people of the house could do to beat it off.

"Whatever has come over the dog?" asked the moujik's old mother. "Why should it hate its master so?"

The moujik told her all that had happened.

"A bad piece of work, my son!" said the old woman. "The dog was disgusted at you not helping it. There it was fighting with the corpse, and you deserted it, and thought only of saving yourself! Now it will owe you a grudge for ever so long."

Next morning, while the family were going about the farmyard, the dog was perfectly quiet. But the moment its master made his appearance, it began to growl like anything. They fastened it to a chain for a whole year , but in spite of that, it never forgot how its master had offended it.

Dog Tails – Canine Fairy Tales, Myths And Legends

The Giant Dog

An Inuit Tale

This tale has been edited and adapted from Knud Rasmussen's book, Eskimo Folk-Tales, published in 1921 by Gyldendal, London & Copenhagen.

There was once a man who had a giant dog. It could swim in the sea, and was so big that it could haul whale and narwhal to shore. The narwhal it would hook on to its side teeth, and swim with them hanging there.

The man who owned it had cut holes in its jaws, and let in thongs through those holes, so that he could make it turn to either side by pulling at the thongs.

And when he and his wife desired to go journeying to any place, they had only to mount on its back.

The man had long wished to have a son, but as none was born to him, he gave his great dog the amulet which his son should have had. This amulet was a knot of hard wood, and the dog was thus made hard to resist the coming of death.

Once the dog ate a man, and then the owner of the dog was forced to leave that place and take land elsewhere. And while he was living in this new place, there came one day a kayak rowing in towards the land, and the man hastened to take up his dog, in case it should eat the stranger. He led it away far up into the hills, and gave it a great bone, that it might have something to gnaw at, and thus be kept busy.

But one day the dog smelt out the stranger, and came down from the hills, and then the man was forced to hide the stranger and his kayak in a far place, in case the dog should tear them in pieces, for it was very fierce.

Now because the dog was so big and fierce, the man had many enemies. And once a stranger came driving in a sledge with three dogs as big as bears, to kill the giant dog. The man went out to meet that sledge, and the dog followed behind him. The dog pretended to be afraid at first, but then, when the stranger's dog set upon it in attack, it turned against them, and crushed the skulls of all three in its teeth.

After a time, the man noticed that his giant dog would go off, now and again, for long journeys in the hills, and would sometimes return with the leg of an inland-dweller. And now he understood that the dog had made it a custom to attack the inland-dwellers and bring back their legs to its master. He could see that the legs were legs of inland-dwellers, for they wore hairy boots.

And it is from this giant dog that the inland-dwellers got their great fear of all dogs. It would always appear suddenly at the window, and drag them out. But it was a good thing that something happened to frighten the inland-dwellers, for they had themselves an evil custom of carrying off lonely folk, especially women, when they had lost their way in the fog.

And that is all I know about the Giant Dog.

The Barghest

An English Tale

This tale is my own version of what's left of a traditional English legend that probably has its roots in old Saxon and Norse storytelling. This tale shares a common grounding with tales such as Gytrash and The Black Dog Of The Pennine Hills.

Once upon a time, in the heart of the Yorkshire moors, there was a small village nestled among the rolling hills and misty valleys. The villagers spoke in hushed tones of the Barghest, a fearsome creature said to haunt the countryside on dark and stormy nights.

Among the villagers was a young shepherd named Thomas, who tended his flock of sheep on the rugged moors. Thomas had heard the tales of the Barghest since he was a boy, but he had never encountered the creature himself. He laughed off the stories, believing them to be nothing more than old wives' tales meant to frighten children.

One evening, as Thomas was leading his sheep back to the village before nightfall, a thick fog descended upon the moors, shrouding everything in an eerie mist. Thomas felt a chill run down his spine as he remembered the stories of the Barghest lurking in the fog.

As he trudged through the mist, Thomas heard a low growl emanating from the darkness. His heart raced as he scanned the shadows, searching for the source of the sound. Suddenly, two glowing eyes appeared in the distance, piercing through the fog like twin orbs of fire.

Thomas's blood ran cold as he realized he was face to face with the Barghest. The creature loomed before him, its black fur bristling, and its sharp teeth bared in a menacing snarl. Thomas felt a wave of terror wash over him as he stood frozen in fear.

But then, to his surprise, the Barghest spoke in a deep, rumbling voice. "Do not be afraid, shepherd," it said. "I mean you no harm."

Thomas blinked in disbelief, unsure if he was dreaming or awake. "What do you want from me?" he asked, his voice trembling.

The Barghest's eyes softened, and it lowered its head. "I seek your help, shepherd," it said. "For I am not the fearsome creature that the villagers believe me to be. I am a guardian of these moors, tasked with protecting them from evil forces that seek to do harm."

Thomas listened intently as the Barghest explained its true nature and the purpose of its presence on the moors. Despite his initial fear, he felt a sense of compassion for the creature and its plight.

Moved by the Barghest's words, Thomas agreed to help. Together, they embarked on a journey to confront the dark forces that threatened the village and the surrounding countryside. Along the way, they faced many trials and challenges, but with courage and determination, they prevailed.

In the end, Thomas realized that the Barghest was not a creature of evil, but a noble guardian fighting to protect the land and its inhabitants. From that day forward, the villagers no longer feared the Barghest, but revered it as a symbol of courage and resilience.

And though the Barghest continued to roam the moors, its presence was no longer feared but welcomed, a reminder that even in the darkest of times, there is always hope and light to guide the way.

The Strange Tale Of Doctor Dog

This story has been adapted from Norman Hinsdale Pitman's version that originally appeared in A Chinese Wonder Book, published in 1919 by E. P. Dutton And Company, New York. A Chinese Wonder Book contains a selection of stories that capture the essence of traditional Chinese culture and storytelling. The book includes tales of magic, dragons, heroes, and supernatural creatures, all woven together with elements of Chinese mythology and folklore.

Far up in the mountains of the Province of Hunan in the central part of China, there once lived in a small village a rich gentleman who had only one child. This girl was the very joy of her father's life.

Now Mr. Min, for that was this gentleman's name, was famous throughout the whole district for his learning, and, as he was also the owner of much property, he spared no effort to teach Honeysuckle the wisdom of the sages, and to give her everything she craved. Of course this was enough to spoil most children, but Honeysuckle was not at all like other children. As sweet as the flower from which she took her name, she listened to her father's slightest command, and obeyed without ever waiting to be told a second time.

Her father often bought kites for her, of every kind and shape. There were fish, birds, butterflies, lizards and huge dragons, one of which had a tail more than thirty feet long. Mr. Min was very skilful in flying these kites for little Honeysuckle, and so naturally did his

239

birds and butterflies circle round and hover about in the air that almost any child would have been deceived and said, "Why, there is a real bird, and not a kite at all!"

Then again, he would fasten a queer little instrument to the string, which made a kind of humming noise, as he waved his hand from side to side. "It is the wind singing, Daddy," cried Honeysuckle, clapping her hands with joy, "singing a kite-song to both of us."

Sometimes, to teach his little darling a lesson if she had been the least naughty, Mr. Min would fasten queerly twisted scraps of paper, on which were written many Chinese words, to the string of her favourite kite.

"What are you doing, Daddy?" Honeysuckle would ask. "What can those queer-looking papers be?"

"On every piece is written a sin that we have done."

"What is a sin, Daddy?"

"Oh, when Honeysuckle has been naughty, that is a sin!" he answered gently. "Your old nurse is afraid to scold you, and if you are to grow up to be a good woman, Daddy must teach you what is right."

Then Mr. Min would send the kite up high, high over the house-tops, even higher than the tall Pagoda on the hillside. When all his cord was let out, he would pick up two sharp stones, and, handing them to Honeysuckle, would say, "Now, daughter, cut the string, and the wind will carry away the sins that are written down on the scraps of paper."

"But, Daddy, the kite is so pretty. Can't we keep our sins a little longer?" she would innocently ask.

"No, child, it is dangerous to hold on to one's sins. Virtue is the foundation of happiness," he would reply sternly, choking back his laughter at her question. "Make haste and cut the cord."

So Honeysuckle, always obedient, at least with her father, would saw the string in two between the sharp stones, and with a childish cry of despair would watch her favourite kite, blown by the wind, sail farther and farther away, until eventually, straining her eyes, she could see it sink slowly to the earth in some far-distant meadow.

"Now laugh and be happy," Mr. Min would say, "for your sins are all gone. See that you don't get a new supply of them."

Honeysuckle was also fond of seeing the Punch and Judy show, for, you must know, this old-fashioned amusement for children was enjoyed by little folks in China, perhaps three thousand years before your great-grandfather was born.

One day when Honeysuckle was sitting inside a shady pavilion that overlooked a tiny fish-pond, she was suddenly seized with a violent attack of colic. Frantic with pain, she told a servant to summon her father, and then without further ado, she fell over in a faint upon the ground.

When Mr. Min reached his daughter's side, she was still unconscious. After sending for the family physician to come post haste, he got his daughter to bed, but although she recovered from her fainting fit, the extreme pain continued until the poor girl was almost dead from exhaustion.

Now, when the learned doctor arrived and peered at her from under his gigantic spectacles, he could not discover the cause of her trouble. However he did not confess his ignorance, but proceeded to prescribe a huge dose of boiling water, to be followed a little later by a compound of pulverized deer's horn and dried toad skin.

Poor Honeysuckle lay in agony for three days, all the time growing weaker and weaker from loss of sleep. Every great doctor in the district had been summoned for consultation, and two had come from Changsha, the chief city of the province, but all to no avail. It was one of those cases that seem to be beyond the power of even the most learned physicians. In the hope of receiving the great reward offered by the desperate father, these wise men searched from cover to cover in the great Chinese Cyclopaedia of Medicine, trying in vain to find a method of treating the unhappy maiden.

Mr. Min sent out a proclamation in every direction, describing his daughter's illness, and offering to bestow on her a handsome dowry and give her in marriage to whoever should be the means of bringing her back to health and happiness. He then sat at her bedside and waited, feeling that he had done all that was in his power. There were many answers to his invitation. Physicians, old and young, came from every part of the Empire to try their skill, and when they had seen poor Honeysuckle and also the huge pile of silver shoes her father offered as a wedding gift, they all fought with might and main for her life, some having been attracted by her great beauty and excellent reputation, others by the tremendous reward.

But, alas for poor Honeysuckle! Not one of all those wise men could cure her! One day, when she was feeling a slight change for the better, she called her father, and, clasping his hand with her tiny one said, "Were it not for your love I would give up this hard fight and pass over into the dark wood, or, as my old grandmother says, fly up into the Western Heavens. For your sake, because I am your only child, and especially because you have no son, I have struggled hard to live, but now I feel that the next attack of that dreadful pain will carry me away. And oh, I do not want to die!"

Here Honeysuckle wept as if her heart would break, and her old father wept too, for the more she suffered the more he loved her.

Just then her face began to turn pale. "It is coming! The pain is coming, father! Very soon I shall be no more. Good-bye, father! Good-bye, good…"

Here her voice broke and a great sob almost broke her father's heart. He turned away from her bedside, for he could not bear to see her suffer. He walked outside and sat down on a rustic bench, his head fell upon his bosom, and the great salt tears trickled down his long grey beard.

As Mr. Min sat there overcome with grief, he was startled at hearing a low whine. Looking up he saw, to his astonishment, a shaggy mountain dog about the size of a Newfoundland. The huge beast looked into the old man's eyes with so intelligent and human an expression, with such a sad and wistful gaze, that the greybeard addressed him, saying, "Why have you come? To cure my daughter?"

The dog replied with three short barks, wagging his tail vigorously and turning toward the half-opened door that led into the room where the girl lay.

By this time, willing to try any chance whatever of reviving his daughter, Mr. Min bade the animal follow him into Honeysuckle's apartment. Placing his forepaws upon the side of her bed, the dog looked long and steadily at the wasted form before him and held his ear intently for a moment over the maiden's heart. Then, with a slight cough he deposited from his mouth into her outstretched hand, a tiny stone. Touching her wrist with his right paw, he motioned to her to swallow the stone.

"Yes, my dear, obey him," counselled her father, as she turned to him inquiringly, "for good Dr. Dog has been sent to your bedside by the mountain fairies, who have heard of your illness and who wish to invite you back to life again."

Without further delay the sick girl, who was by this time almost burned away by the fever, raised her hand to her lips and swallowed the tiny charm. Wonder of wonders! No sooner had it passed her lips than a miracle occurred. The red flush passed away from her face, the pulse resumed its normal beat, the pains departed from her body, and she arose from the bed well and smiling.

Flinging her arms about her father's neck, she cried out in joy, "Oh, I am well again, well and happy, thanks to the medicine of the good physician."

The noble dog barked three times, wild with delight at hearing these tearful words of gratitude, bowed low, and put his nose in Honeysuckle's outstretched hand.

Mr. Min, greatly moved by his daughter's magical recovery, turned to the strange physician, saying, "Noble Sir, were it not for the form you have taken, for some unknown reason, I would willingly give four times the sum in silver that I promised for the cure of the girl, into your possession. As it is, I suppose you have no use for silver, but remember that so long as we live, whatever we have is yours for the asking, and I beg of you to prolong your visit, to make this the home of your old age. In short, remain here for ever as my guest, nay, as a member of my family."

The dog barked thrice, as if in assent. From that day he was treated as an equal by father and daughter. The many servants were commanded to obey his slightest whim, to serve him with the most expensive food on the market, to spare no expense in making him the happiest and best-fed dog in all the world. Day after day he ran at Honeysuckle's side as she gathered flowers in her garden, lay down before her door when she was resting, and guarded her Sedan chair when she was carried by servants into the city. In short, they were constant companions, and a stranger would have thought they had been friends from childhood.

One day, however, just as they were returning from a journey outside her father's compound, at the very instant when Honeysuckle was alighting from her chair, without a moment's warning, the huge animal dashed past the attendants, seized his beautiful mistress in his mouth, and before anyone could stop him, bore her off to the mountains. By the time the alarm was sounded, darkness had fallen over the valley and as the night was cloudy no trace could be found of the dog and his fair burden.

Once more the frantic father left no stone unturned to save his daughter. Huge rewards were offered, bands of woodmen scoured the mountains high and low, but, alas, no sign of the girl could be found! The unfortunate father gave up the search and began to prepare himself for the grave. There was nothing now left in life that he cared for, nothing but thoughts of his departed daughter. Honeysuckle was gone for ever.

"Alas!" he said, quoting the lines of a famous poet who had fallen into despair:

"My whiting hair would make an endless rope,
Yet would not measure all my depth of woe."

Several long years passed by. These were years of sorrow for the ageing man, pining for his departed daughter. One beautiful October day he was sitting in the very same pavilion where he had so often sat with his darling. His head was bowed forward on his breast, and his forehead was lined with grief. A rustling of leaves attracted his attention. He looked up. Standing directly in front of him was Dr. Dog, and there, riding on his back, clinging to the animal's shaggy hair, was Honeysuckle, his long-lost daughter, while standing nearby were three of the handsomest boys he had ever set eyes upon!

"Ah, my daughter! My darling daughter, where have you been all these years?" cried the delighted father, pressing the girl to his aching breast. "Have you suffered many a cruel pain since you were snatched away so suddenly? Has your life been filled with sorrow?"

"Only at the thought of your grief," she replied, tenderly, stroking his forehead with her slender fingers, "only at the thought of your suffering, only at the thought of how I should like to see you every day and tell you that my husband was kind and good to me. For you must know, dear father, this is no mere animal that stands beside you. This Dr. Dog, who cured me and claimed me as his bride because of your promise, is a great magician. He can change himself at will into a thousand shapes. He chooses to come here in the form of a mountain beast so that no one may penetrate the secret of his distant palace."

"Then he is your husband?" faltered the old man, gazing at the animal with a new expression on his wrinkled face.

"Yes, my kind and noble husband, the father of my three sons, your grandchildren, whom we have brought to pay you a visit."

"And where do you live?"

"In a wonderful cave in the heart of the great mountains, a beautiful cave whose walls and floors are covered with crystals, and encrusted with sparkling gems. The chairs and tables are set with jewels, the rooms are lighted by a thousand glittering diamonds. Oh, it is lovelier than the palace of the Son of Heaven himself! We feed on the flesh of wild deer and mountain goats, and fish from the clearest mountain stream. We drink cold water out of golden goblets, without first boiling it, for it is purity itself. We breathe fragrant air that blows through forests of pine and hemlock. We live only to love each other and our children, and oh, we are so happy! And you, father, you must come back with us to the great mountains and live there with us the rest of your days, which, the gods grant, may be very many."

The old man pressed his daughter once more to his breast and embraced the children, who clambered over him rejoicing at the discovery of a grandfather they had never seen before.

From Dr. Dog and his fair Honeysuckle are sprung, it is said, the well-known race of people called the Yus, who even now inhabit the mountainous regions of the Canton and Hunan provinces. It is not for this reason, however, that we have told the story here, but because we felt sure every reader would like to learn the secret of the dog that cured a sick girl and won her for his bride.

A Brave Dog

An Original Tale By Sir Samuel W. Baker

This tale has been edited and adapted from William Patten's collection, The Junior Classics, Volume 8, Animal Tales, and illustrated by Harold Nelson. The book was published in 1912 by. P. F. Collier & Son, New York.

When I was a boy, my grandfather frequently told a story concerning a dog which he knew, as a more than ordinary example of the fidelity so frequently exhibited by the race. This animal was a mastiff that belonged to an intimate friend, to whom it was a constant companion. It was an enormous specimen of that well-known breed, which is not generally celebrated for any peculiar intelligence, but is chiefly remarkable for size and strength. This dog had been brought up by its master from puppyhood, and as the proprietor was a single man, there had been no division of affection, as there would have been had the dog belonged to a family of several members. Turk regarded nobody but his owner.

Whenever Mr. Prideaux went out for a walk, Turk was sure to be near his heels. Street dogs would bark and snarl at the giant as his massive form attracted their attention, but Turk seldom condescended to notice such vulgar demonstrations, for he was a noble-looking creature, somewhat resembling a small lioness, but although he was gentle and quiet in disposition, he had upon several occasions been provoked beyond endurance, and his attack had been nearly always fatal to his assailants. He slept at night outside his master's door, and no sentry could be more alert upon his watch than the faithful dog, who had apparently only one ambition - to protect, and to accompany his owner.

Mr. Prideaux had a dinner-party. He never invited ladies, but simply entertained his friends as a bachelor; his dinners were but secondary to the quality of his guests, however, who were always men of reputation either in the literary world, or in the modern annals of society. The dog Turk was invariably present, and usually stretched his huge form upon the hearth-rug.

It was a cold night in winter, when Mr. Prideaux's friends were talking after dinner, that the conversation turned upon the subject of dogs. Almost every person had an anecdote to relate, and my own grandfather being present, had no doubt added his mite to the collection, when Turk suddenly awoke from a sound sleep, and having stretched himself until he appeared to be awake to the situation, walked up to his master's side, and rested his large head upon the table.

"Ha ha, Turk!" exclaimed Mr. Prideaux, "you must have heard our arguments about the dogs, so you have put in an appearance."

"And a magnificent specimen he is!" remarked my grandfather; "but although a mastiff is the largest and most imposing of the race, I do not think it is as sensible as many others."

"As a rule you are right," replied his master, "because they are generally chained up as watch-dogs, and have not the intimate association with human beings which is so great an advantage to house-dogs, but Turk has been my constant companion from the first month of his existence, and his intelligence is very remarkable. He understands most things that I say, if they are connected with himself. He will often lie upon the rug with his large eyes fixed upon me as though searching my inward thoughts, and he will frequently be aware instinctively that I wish to go out, and upon such times he will fetch my hat, cane, or gloves, whichever may be at hand, and wait for me at the front door. He will take a letter or any other token to several houses of my acquaintance, and wait for a reply, and he can perform a variety of actions that would imply a share of reason seldom possessed by other dogs."

A smile of incredulity upon several faces was at once perceived by Mr. Prideaux, who immediately took a guinea from his pocket, and addressed his dog. "Here, Turk! They won't believe in you, so, take this guinea to Mr. Wallace, and bring me a receipt."

The dog wagged his huge tail with evident pleasure, and the guinea having been placed in his mouth, he hastened towards the door. When this was opened, he was admitted through the front entrance to the street. It was a miserable night, for the wind was blowing the sleet and rain against the windows, the gutters were running with muddy water, and the weather was exactly that which is expressed by the common term, "not fit to turn a dog out in." Nevertheless, Turk had started upon his mission in the howling gale and darkness, while the front door was once more closed against the blast.

The party were comfortably seated around the fire, and much interested in the success or failure of the dog's adventure.

"How long will it be before we may expect Turk's return?" inquired an incredulous guest.

"The house to which I have sent him is about a mile and a half distant, therefore if there is no delay when he barks for admission at the door, and my friend is not absent from home, he should return in about three-quarters of an hour with an acknowledgment. If, on the other hand, he cannot gain admission, he may wait for any length of time," replied his master.

Bets were exchanged among the company. Some supported the dog's chances of success, while others were against him.

The evening wore away, the allotted time was exceeded, and a whole hour had passed, but no dog had returned. Fresh bets were made, but the odds were against the dog. His master was still hopeful.

"I must tell you," said Mr. Prideaux, "that Turk frequently carries notes for me, and as he knows the house well, he certainly will not make a mistake. Perhaps my friend may be dining out, in which case Turk will probably wait for a longer time."

Two hours passed. The storm was raging. Mr. Prideaux himself went to the front door, which flew open before a fierce gust the instant that the lock was turned. The clouds were rushing past a moon but faintly visible at short intervals, and the gutters were clogged with masses of half-melted snow. "Poor Turk!" muttered his master, "this is indeed a wretched night for you. Perhaps they have kept you in the warm kitchen, and will not allow you to return in such fearful weather."

When Mr. Prideaux returned to his guests he could not conceal his disappointment. "Ha!" exclaimed one who had betted against the dog, "I never doubted his sagacity. With a guinea in his mouth, he has probably gone into some house of entertainment where dogs are supplied with dinner and a warm bed, instead of shivering in a winter's gale!"

Jokes were made by the winners of bets at the absent dog's expense, but his master was anxious and annoyed. The various bets were paid by the losers, and poor Turk's reputation had suffered severely. It was long past midnight, and the guests were departed, the storm was raging, and violent gusts occasionally shook the house. Mr. Prideaux was alone in his study, and he poked the fire until it blazed and roared up the chimney.

"What can have become of that dog?" exclaimed his master to himself, now really anxious; "I hope they kept him. Most likely they would not send him back upon such a dreadful night."

Mr. Prideaux's study was close to the front door, and his acute attention was suddenly directed to a violent shaking and scratching, accompanied by a prolonged whine. In an instant he ran into the hall, and unlocked the entrance door. A mass of filth and mud entered. This was Turk!

The dog seemed dreadfully fatigued, and was shivering with wet and cold. His usually clean coat was thick with mire, as though he had been dragged through deep mud. He wagged his tail when he heard his master's voice, but appeared dejected and ill.

Mr. Prideaux had rung the bell, and the servants, who were equally interested as their master in Turk's failure to perform his mission, had attended the summons. The dog was taken downstairs, and immediately placed in a large tub of hot water, in which he was accustomed to be bathed. It was now discovered that in addition to mud and dirt, which almost concealed his coat, he was smeared with blood!

Mr. Prideaux himself sponged his favourite with hot soap and water, and, to his astonishment, he perceived wounds of a serious nature. The dog's throat was badly torn, his back and breast were deeply bitten, and there could be no doubt that he had been worried by a pack of dogs. This was a strange occurrence, that Turk should be discomfited!

He was now washed clean, and was being rubbed dry with a thick towel while he stood upon a blanket before the kitchen fire. "Why, Turk, old boy, what has been the matter? Tell us all about it, poor old man!" exclaimed his master.

The dog was now thoroughly warmed, and he panted with the heat of the kitchen fire; he opened his mouth, and the guinea which he had received in trust dropped on the kitchen floor!

"There is some mystery in this," said Mr. Prideaux, "which I will endeavour to discover tomorrow. He has been set upon by strange dogs, and rather than lose the guinea, he has allowed himself to be half killed without once opening his mouth in self-defence! Poor Turk!" continued his master, "You must have lost your way, old man, in the darkness and storm, most likely confused after the unequal fight. What an example you have given us wretched humans in being steadfast to a trust!"

Turk was wonderfully better after his warm bath. He lapped up a large bowl of good thick soup mixed with bread, and in half an hour was comfortably asleep upon his thick rug by his master's bedroom door.

By the following morning the storm had cleared away, and a bright sky had succeeded to the gloom of the preceding night.

Immediately after breakfast, Mr. Prideaux, accompanied by his dog (who was, although rather stiff, not much the worse for the rough treatment he had received), started for a walk towards the house to which he had directed Turk upon the previous evening. He was anxious to discover whether his friend had been absent, as he concluded that the dog might have been waiting for admittance, and had been perhaps attacked by some dogs belonging to the house, or its neighbours'.

The master and Turk had walked for nearly a mile, and had just turned the corner of a street when, as they passed a butcher's shop upon the right hand, a large brindled mastiff rushed from the shop-door, and flew at Turk with unprovoked ferocity.

"Call your dog off!" shouted Mr. Prideaux to the butcher, who surveyed the attack with impudent satisfaction. "Call him off, or my dog will kill him!" continued Mr. Prideaux.

The usually docile Turk had rushed to meet his assailant with a fury that was extraordinary. With a growl like that of a lion, he quickly seized his antagonist by the throat. Rearing upon his hind legs, he exerted his tremendous strength, and in a fierce struggle of only a few seconds, he threw the brindled dog upon its back. It was in vain that Mr. Prideaux endeavoured to call him off for the rage of his favourite was quite ungovernable. He never for an instant relaxed his hold, but with the strength of a wild beast of prey, Turk shook the head of the butcher's dog to the right and left until it struck each time heavily against the pavement. The butcher attempted to interfere, and lashed him with a huge whip.

"Stand clear! Fair play! Don't you strike my dog!" shouted Mr. Prideaux. "Your dog was the first to attack!"

In reply to the whip, Turk had redoubled his fury, and, without relinquishing his hold, he had now dragged the butcher's dog off the pavement, and occasionally shaking the body as he pulled the unresisting mass along the gutter, he drew it into the middle of the street.

A large crowd had collected, which completely stopped the thoroughfare. There were no police in those days, but only watchmen, who were few and far between. Even had they been present, it is probable they would have joined in the amusement of a dog-fight, which in that age of brutality was considered to be sport.

"Fair play!" shouted the bystanders. "Let 'em have it out!" cried others, as they formed a circle around the dogs. In the meantime, Mr. Prideaux had seized Turk by his collar, while the butcher was endeavouring to release the remains of his dog from the infuriated and deadly grip..

At length Mr. Prideaux's voice and action appeared for a moment to create a calm, and, snatching the opportunity, he, with the assistance of a person in the crowd, held back his dog, as the carcass of the butcher's dog was dragged away by the lately insolent owner. The dog was dead!

Turk's flanks were heaving with the intense exertion and excitement of the fight, and he strained to escape from his master's hold to once more attack the lifeless body of his late antagonist.. At length, by kind words and the caress of the well-known hand, his fury was calmed down..

"Well, that's the most curious adventure I've ever had with a dog!" exclaimed the butcher, who was now completely crestfallen. "Why, that's the very dog! He is so... That's the very dog who came by my shop late last night in the howling storm, and my dog Tiger went at him and towzled him up completely. I never saw such a cowardly cur. He wouldn't show any fight, although he was pretty near as big as a costermonger's donkey, and there my dog Tiger nearly ate half of him, and dragged the other half about the gutter, till he looked more like an old door-mat than a dog, and I thought he must have killed him, and here he comes out as fresh as paint today, and kills old Tiger clean off as though he'd been only a biggish cat!"

"What do you say?" asked Mr. Prideaux. "Was it your dog that worried my poor dog last night, when he was upon a message of trust?. My friend, I thank you for this communication, but let me inform you of the fact that my dog had a guinea in his mouth to carry to my friend, and rather than drop it he allowed himself to be half killed by your savage Tiger. Today he has proved his courage, and your dog has discovered his mistake. This is the guinea that he dropped from his mouth when he returned to me after midnight, beaten and distressed!" said Mr. Prideaux, much excited. "Here, Turk, old boy, take the guinea again, and come along with me! You have had your revenge, and have given us all a lesson."

His master gave him the guinea in his mouth, and they continued their walk.. It appeared, upon Mr. Prideaux's arrival at his friend's house, that Turk had never been there. Probably after his defeat he had become so confused that he lost his way in the heavy storm, and had at length regained the road home sometime after midnight, in the deplorable condition already described.

Parson Puss And Parson Dog

A Jamaican Tale

This story has been adapted from Walter Jekyll's version that originally appeared in Jamaican Song and Story, published in 1901 by The Folk-lore Society & David Nutt, London.

One day, Toad had been courting a very pretty Indian girl for a long time, but he didn't want to marry her. He preferred to live with her without getting married.

Puss, who was the parson, was involved in the situation. Toad's mother called Puss, and when he arrived, she explained the situation to him. Puss considered Toad to be one of his beloved church members, and he didn't want Toad to leave his church. Puss talked to Toad until he agreed to marry the girl.

However, Dog was also a parson. Toad sent invitations to all his friends and relatives, including Tacoma and his family, as well as Mr. Anancy and his family. Toad also invited Parson Dog to the wedding.

On the day of the wedding, Parson Puss arrived to officiate the ceremony. Parson Dog also came, wearing his gown and intending to take over the ceremony. But Toad insisted that he preferred his own parson. Dog threatened that there might be a fight if he didn't get to conduct the ceremony, but Puss's wife, who was the organ-player, dismissed Dog's threats.

Puss assured Toad's mother-in-law not to worry about Dog's attempts to interfere, as Dog was known for being unreliable. Eventually, Dog left.

After Dog left, Puss married off Toad. Once the cake was finished, Puss suggested that the young ladies play a game in a ring, and they agreed.

Meanwhile, Dog was unaware of what was happening until he heard a song mocking him. He became angry and confronted Puss, starting a fight. Puss, realizing Dog was stronger, climbed a tall tree to save himself.

Since that day, Dog and Puss have never been able to reconcile.

How The Dog Outwitted The Leopard

An African Tale

This tale has been edited and adapted from Henry Morton Stanley's book, My Dark Companions, *published in 1893 by Sampson, Lowe, Marston and Company, London.*

In the early time there was a dog and a leopard dwelling together in a cave like chums. They shared and fared alike. Exact half of everything and equal effort were the terms upon which they lived. They made many a famous raid among the flocks and fowls in the human villages. The leopard was by far the strongest and boldest, and was most successful in catching prey. Dog lived so well on the spoils brought home by his friend that he became at last fat and lazy, and he began to dislike going out at night in the rain and cold dew, and to hide this growing habit from Leopard he had to be very cunning. He always invented some excuse or another to explain why he brought nothing to the common larder, and finally he hit upon a new plan of saving himself from the toil and danger.

Just before dusk one day, Leopard and Dog were sociably chatting together, when Leopard said that he intended that night to catch a fine fat black goat which he had observed in the nearest village to their den. He had watched him getting fatter every day, and he was bent upon bringing him home.

"Black is it?" cried Dog. "That is strange, for that is also the colour of the one I want to catch tonight."

The two friends slept until most of the night was gone, but when there were signs that morning was not far off they silently loped away to their work.

They parted at the village which Leopard had selected to rob, Dog whispering "Good luck" to him. Dog trotted off a little way and sneaked back to watch his friend.

Leopard stealthily surveying the tall fence, saw one place which he could leap over, and at one spring was inside the village. Snuffing about, he discovered the goat-pen, forced an entrance, and seizing his prize by the neck, drew it out. He then flung it over his shoulders, and with a mighty leap landed outside the fence.

Dog, who had watched his chance, now cried out in an affected voice, "Hi, hi, wake up! Leopard has killed the goat. There he is. Ah, ah! Kill him, kill him!"

Alarmed at the noise made, and hearing a rustle in the grass near him, Leopard was obliged to abandon his prize, and to save his own life, dropped the goat and fled.

Dog, chuckling loudly at the success of his ruse, picked the dead goat up, and trotted home to the den with it.

"Oh, see, Leopard!" cried he, as he reached the entrance, "What a fat goat I've got at my village. Is it not a heavy one? But where is yours? Did you not succeed after all?"

"Oh! I was alarmed by the owners in the village, who pursued me and yelled out, `Kill him, kill him!' and there was something rustling in the grass close by, and I thought that I was done for, but I dropped the goat and ran away. I dare say they have found the animal by now, and have eaten our meat. Never mind, though, better luck next time. I saw a fine fat white goat in the pen, which I am sure to catch tomorrow night."

"Well, I am very sorry, but cheer your heart. You shall have an equal share with me of this. Let us stir ourselves to cook it."

They gathered sticks and made a fire, and began to roast it. When it was nearly ready Dog went outside, and took a stick and beat the ground, and whined out, "Oh! Please, I did not do it. It was Leopard that killed the goat. Oh! Don't kill me. It was Leopard who stole it."

Leopard, hearing these cries and the blows of the stick, thought to himself, "Ah! The men have followed us to our den, and are killing Dog. Then they will come and kill me if I do not run." He therefore ran out and escaped.

Dog, on seeing him well away, coolly returned to the den and devoured the whole of the meat, leaving only the bones.

After a long time Leopard returned to the den, and found Dog moaning piteously. "What is the matter, my friend?" he asked.

"Ah! Oh! Don't touch me. Don't touch me, I beg of you. I am so bruised and sore all over! Ah! My bones! They have half killed me," moaned Dog.

"Poor fellow! Well, lie still and rest. There is nothing like rest for a bruised body. I will get that white goat the next time I try."

After waiting two or three days, Leopard departed to obtain the white goat. Dog sneaked after him, and served his friend in the same way, bringing the white goat himself, and bragging how he had succeeded, while pretending to pity Leopard for his bad luck.

Three times running Dog served him with the same trick, and Leopard was much mortified at his own failure. Then Leopard thought of the Muzimu, the oracle who knows all things, and gives such good advice to those who are unfortunate and ask for his help, and he resolved, in his distress, to seek him.

In the heart of the tall, dark woods, where the bush is most dense, where vines clamber over the clumps, and fold themselves round and round the trees, and hang in long coils by the side of a cool stream, the Muzimu resided.

Leopard softly drew near the sacred place and cried, "Oh! Muzimu, have pity on me. I am almost dying with hunger. I used to be bold and strong, and successful, but now, of late, though I catch my prey as of old, something always happens to scare me away, and I lose the meat I have taken. Help me, O Muzimu, and tell how my good luck may return."

After a while the Muzimu answered in a deep voice, "Leopard, your ill-luck comes from your own folly. You know how to catch prey, but it takes a dog to know how to eat it. Go. Watch your friend, and your ill-luck will fly away."

Leopard was never very wise, though he had good eyes, and was swift and brave, and he thought over what the Muzimu said. He could not understand in what way his good luck would return by watching his friend, but he resolved to follow the advice of the Muzimu.

The next night Leopard gave out that he was going to seize a dun-coloured goat, and Dog said, "Ah! That is what I mean to do too. I think a dun-coated goat so sweet."

The village was reached, a low place was found in the palings, and Leopard, as quick as you could wink, was over and among the goats. With one stroke he struck his victim dead, threw it over his shoulders, and, with a flying leap, carried it outside. Dog, who was hiding near the place, in a strange voice cried, "Ah! Here he is, the thief of a Leopard! Kill him! Kill him!"

Leopard turning his head around, saw Dog in the grass and heard him yelp, "Awu-ou-ou! Awu-ou-ou! Kill him! Kill him!"

Leopard dropped the goat for an instant and said, "Ah, it is you, my false friend, is it? Wait a bit, and I will teach you how you may steal once too often."

With eyes like balls of fire, he rushed at him, and would have torn him into pieces, but Dog's instinct told him that the game he had been playing was up, and burying his tail between his hind legs, he turned and fled for dear life. Round and round the village he ran, darting this way and that, until, finding his strength was oozing out of him, he dashed finally through a gap in the fence, straight into a man's house and under the bed, where he lay gasping and panting. Seeing that the man, who had been scared by his sudden entry, was about to take his spear to kill him, he crawled from under the bed to the man's feet, and licked them, and turned on his back imploring mercy. The man took pity on him, tied him up, and made a pet of him.

Ever since Dog and Man have been firm friends, but a mortal hatred has existed between Dog and Leopard. Dog's back always bristles straight up when his enemy is about, and there is no truer warning of the Leopard's presence than that given by Dog, while Leopard would rather eat a dog than a goat any day. That is the way, as I heard it in Unyoro, that the chumship between Leopard and Dog was broken up.

The Wolf And The Dog

A Cherokee Tale

This tale has been edited and adapted from Katharine Berry Judson's book, Myths and Legends of the Mississippi Valley and the Great Lakes, published in 1914 by A. C. McClurg And Co., Chicago.

In the beginning, so they say, Dog was put on the mountain side and Wolf beside the fire. When winter came, Dog could not stand the cold, and drove Wolf away from the fire. Wolf ran into the mountains and he liked it so well that he has stayed there ever since.

Gytrash

An English Tale

This tale is my own version of a traditional English legend that probably has its roots in old Saxon and Norse storytelling. This tale shares a common grounding with tales such as The Barghest and The Black Dog Of The Pennine Hills.

In the heart of the English countryside, where ancient forests whispered secrets and misty moors stretched as far as the eye could see, there roamed a mysterious creature known as the Gytrash. This spectral dog, with eyes like burning coals and fur as dark as the midnight sky, was said to haunt the lonely roads and shadowy lanes of the countryside.

Legend had it that the Gytrash was a shape-shifter, able to take on various forms to lure unsuspecting travellers astray. Some claimed it appeared as a massive hound, while others whispered of a spectral horse or even a hooded figure cloaked in darkness.

Among the villagers who lived near the haunted moors was a young shepherd named Thomas. Thomas had heard the stories of the Gytrash since he was a boy, but he had never encountered the creature himself. He scoffed at the tales, believing them to be nothing more than old wives' superstitions meant to scare children.

One moonlit night, as Thomas was tending his flock of sheep on the edge of the moors, he heard a strange howling echoing through the darkness. His heart skipped a beat as he realized it was the sound of the Gytrash, the creature he had dismissed as mere legend.

Fearful yet curious, Thomas followed the eerie howling deeper into the moors, his lantern casting shadows on the mist-covered ground. As he ventured further from the safety of the village, the howling grew louder, echoing off the ancient stones and gnarled trees.

Suddenly, Thomas stumbled upon a clearing bathed in moonlight, and there, standing before him, was the Gytrash. The creature loomed before him, its eyes gleaming with an otherworldly light, and Thomas felt a chill run down his spine.

But to his surprise, the Gytrash did not attack. Instead, it regarded him with an almost human expression, as if it were trying to communicate something. Thomas felt a sense of empathy for the creature, sensing that it was not the malevolent force that the villagers believed it to be.

Trembling, Thomas reached out to touch the Gytrash, expecting to feel icy fur or cold stone. To his amazement, the creature nuzzled his hand, its touch warm and comforting despite its eerie appearance.

In that moment, Thomas realized that the Gytrash was not a creature of darkness, but a lost soul seeking companionship in the lonely moors. Moved by compassion, he offered the Gytrash food and shelter, welcoming it into his life with open arms.

From that day forth, Thomas and the Gytrash became unlikely friends, roaming the moors together and sharing in each other's company. And though the villagers continued to fear the spectral dog, Thomas knew in his heart that the Gytrash was not a creature to be feared but a loyal companion and guardian of the moors.

And so, the legend of the Gytrash lived on, a testament to the power of friendship and understanding in a deceiving world.

The Little Hunting Dog

A Chinese Tale

This story has been adapted from Dr. Richard Wilhelm's version that originally appeared in The Chinese Fairy Book, published in 1921 by Frederick A. Stokes Company, New York. Wilhelm's translations aimed to capture the essence of the original Chinese texts while making them accessible to English-speaking audiences. His deep understanding of Chinese language and culture shone through in his translations, allowing readers to appreciate the beauty and depth of these timeless tales.

ONCE upon a time, in the city of Shansi, there lived a scholar who found the company of others too noisy for him. So he made his home in a Buddhist temple. Yet he suffered because there were always so many gnats and fleas in his room that he could not sleep at night.

Once he was resting on his bed after dinner, when suddenly two little knights with plumes in their helmets rode into the room. They might have been two inches high, and rode horses about the size of grasshoppers. On their gauntleted hands they held hunting falcons as large as flies. They rode about the room with great rapidity. The scholar had no more than set eyes on them when a third entered, clad like the others, but carrying a bow and arrows and leading a little hunting dog the size of an ant with him. After him came a great throng of footmen and horsemen, several hundred in all. And they had hunting falcons and hunting dogs by the hundred, too. Then the fleas and gnats began to rise in the air, but were all slain by the falcons. And the hunting dogs climbed on the bed, and sniffed along the walls trailing the fleas, and ate them up. They followed the trace of whatever hid in the cracks, and nosed it out, so that in a short space of time they had killed nearly all the vermin.

The scholar pretended to be asleep and watched them. And the falcons settled down on him, and the dogs crawled along his body. Shortly after came a man clad in yellow, wearing a king's crown, who climbed on an empty couch and seated himself there. And at once all the horsemen rode up, descended from their horses and brought him all the birds and game. They then gathered beside him in a great throng, and conversed with him in a strange tongue.

Not long after the king got into a small chariot and his bodyguards saddled their horses with the greatest rapidity. Then they galloped out with great cries of homage, till it looked as though some one were scattering beans and a heavy cloud of dust rose behind them.

They had nearly all of them disappeared, while the scholar's eyes were still fixed on them full of terror and astonishment, and he could not imagine where they had come from. He slipped on his shoes and looked, but they had vanished without a trace. Then he returned and looked all about his room, but there was nothing to be seen. Only, on a brick against the wall, they had forgotten a little hunting dog. The scholar quickly caught it and found it quite tame. He put it in his paint-box and examined it closely. It had a very smooth, fine coat, and wore a little collar around its neck. He tried to feed it a few bread-crumbs, but the little dog only sniffed at them and let them lie. Then it leaped into the bed and hunted up some nits and gnats in the folds of the linen, which it devoured. Then it returned and lay down. When the night had passed the scholar feared it might have run away, but there it lay, curled up as before. Whenever the scholar went to bed, the dog climbed into it and bit to death any vermin it could find. Not a fly or gnat dared alight while it was around. The scholar loved it like a prized jewel.

But once he took a nap in the daytime, and the little dog crawled into bed beside him. The scholar woke and turned around, supporting himself on his side. As he did so he felt something, and feared it might be his little dog. He quickly rose and looked, but it was already dead - pressed flat, as though cut out of paper!

But at any rate none of the vermin had survived it.

Dog Tails – Canine Fairy Tales, Myths And Legends

The Elephant And The Dog

An African Tale

This tale has been edited and adapted from Ellen C. Babbitt's book, More Jakata Tales, published in 1922 by The Century Company.

Once upon a time a Dog used to go into the stable where the king's Elephant lived. At first the Dog went there to get the food that was left after the Elephant had finished eating.

Day after day the Dog went to the stable, waiting around for bits to eat. By and by the Elephant and the Dog came to be great friends. Then the Elephant began to share his food with the Dog, and they ate together. When the Elephant slept, his friend the Dog slept beside him. When the Elephant felt like playing, he would catch the Dog in his trunk and swing him to and fro. Neither the Dog nor the Elephant was quite happy unless the other was nearby.

One day a farmer saw the Dog and said to the Elephant-keeper: "I will buy that Dog. He looks good-tempered, and I see that he is smart. How much do you want for the Dog?"

The Elephant-keeper did not care for the Dog, and he did want some money just then. So he asked a fair price, and the farmer paid it and took the Dog away to the country.

The king's Elephant missed the Dog and did not care to eat when his friend was not there to share the food. When the time came for the Elephant to bathe, he would not bathe. The next day again the

Elephant would not eat, and he would not bathe. The third day, when the Elephant would neither eat nor bathe, the king was told about it.

The king sent for his chief servant, saying, "Go to the stable and find out why the Elephant is acting in this way."

The chief servant went to the stable and looked the Elephant all over. Then he said to the Elephant-keeper: "There seems to be nothing the matter with this Elephant's body, but why does he look so sad? Has he lost a playmate?"

"Yes," said the keeper, "there was a Dog who ate and slept and played with the Elephant. The Dog went away three days ago."

"Do you know where the Dog is now?" asked the chief servant.

"No, I do not," said the keeper.

Then the chief servant went back to the king and said, "The Elephant is not sick, but he is lonely without his friend, the Dog."

"Where is the Dog?" asked the king.

"A farmer took him away, so the Elephant-keeper says," said the chief servant. "No one knows where the farmer lives."

"Very well," said the king. "I will send word all over the country, asking the man who bought this Dog to turn him loose. I will give him back as much as he paid for the Dog."

When the farmer who had bought the Dog heard this, he turned him loose. The Dog ran back as fast as ever he could go to the Elephant's stable. The Elephant was so glad to see the Dog that he picked him up with his trunk and put him on his head. Then he put him down again.

When the Elephant-keeper brought food, the Elephant watched the Dog as he ate, and then took his own food. All the rest of their lives the Elephant and the Dog lived together.

Why Dogs Wag their Tails

A Visayan , Philippines Tale

This story has been adapted from Mabel Cook Cole's version that originally appeared in Philippine Folk Tales, published in 19161 by A. C. McClurg & Co., Chicago.

A rich man in a certain town once owned a dog and a cat, both of which were very useful to him. The dog had served his master for many years and had become so old that he had lost his teeth and was unable to fight any more, but he was a good guide and companion to the cat who was strong and cunning.

The master had a daughter who was attending school at a convent some distance from home, and very often he sent the dog and the cat with presents to the girl.

One day he called the faithful animals and bade them carry a magic ring to his daughter.

"You are strong and brave," he said to the cat "You may carry the ring, but you must be careful not to drop it"

And to the dog he said, "You must accompany the cat to guide her and keep her from harm."

They promised to do their best, and started out. All went well until they came to a river. As there was neither bridge nor boat, there was no way to cross but to swim.

"Let me take the magic ring," said the dog as they were about to plunge into the water.

"Oh, no," replied the cat, "the master gave it to me to carry."

"But you cannot swim well," argued the dog. "I am strong and can take good care of it."

But the cat refused to give up the ring until finally the dog threatened to kill her, and then she reluctantly gave it to him.

The river was wide and the water so swift that they grew very tired, and just before they reached the opposite bank the dog dropped the ring. They searched carefully, but could not find it anywhere, and after a while they turned back to tell their master of the sad loss. Just before reaching the house, however, the dog was so overcome with fear that he turned and ran away and never was seen again.

The cat went on alone, and when the master saw her coming he called out to know why she had returned so soon and what had become of her companion. The poor cat was frightened, but as well as she could she explained how the ring had been lost and how the dog had run away.

On hearing her story the master was very angry, and commanded that all his people should search for the dog, and that it should be punished by having its tail cut off.

He also ordered that all the dogs in the world should join in the search, and ever since when one dog meets another he says: "Are you the old dog that lost the magic ring? If so, your tail must be cut off." Then immediately each shows his teeth and wags his tail to prove that he is not the guilty one.

Since then, too, cats have been afraid of water and will not swim across a river if they can avoid it.

Why Mr. Dog Runs Brother Rabbit

An African American Folklore Tale

This tale has been edited and adapted from Joel Chandler Harris's book, Nights With Uncle Remus, published in 1883 by Houghton Mifflin Company, Boston and New York.

There was a time when old Brer Rabbit had to go to town for something for his family, and he was almost ashamed to go because his shoes were completely worn out. But he had to go, so he put on a brave face and took his walking stick and set off as boldly as the next one.

Well, old Brer Rabbit went on down the road until he came to the place where some folks had camped out the night before, and he sat down by the fire to warm his feet because the mornings were kind of cold, like these mornings. He sat there looking at his toes, and he felt very sorry for himself.

He sat there, and it wasn't long before he heard something trotting down the road, and he looked up and there came Mr. Dog, sniffing around to see if the folks had left any scraps by their campfire. Mr. Dog was all dressed up in his Sunday best, and more than that, he had on a pair of brand new shoes.

When Brer Rabbit saw those shoes, he felt very bad, but he didn't show it. He bowed to Mr. Dog very politely, and Mr. Dog bowed back, because they were old acquaintances. Brer Rabbit said, "Mr. Dog, where are you going all dressed up like this?"

"I'm going to town, Brer Rabbit; where are you going?"

"I thought I'd go to town myself to get a new pair of shoes, because my old ones are worn out and they hurt my feet so bad I can't wear them. Those are very nice shoes you have on, Mr. Dog; where did you get them?"

"Down in town, Brer Rabbit, down in town."

"They fit you very nicely, Mr. Dog, and I wish you would be so kind as to let me try one of them on."

Brer Rabbit spoke so sweetly that Mr. Dog sat right down on the ground and took off one of the back shoes and lent it to Brer Rabbit. Brer Rabbit hopped off down the road and then he came back. He told Mr. Dog that the shoe fitted very nicely, but with just one of them on, it made him trot sideways.

Mr. Dog pulled off the other back shoe, and Brer Rabbit trotted off to try it. He came back and said, "They're very nice, Mr. Dog, but they kind of lift me up behind, and I don't exactly know how they feel."

This made Mr. Dog want to be polite, so he took off the front shoes, and Brer Rabbit put them on and stomped his feet, saying, "Now that feels like shoes," and he trotted off down the road, and when he should have turned around, he just laid back his ears and kept on going, and it wasn't long before he was out of sight.

Mr. Dog called and told him to come back, but Brer Rabbit just kept going. Mr. Dog called, but Mr. Rabbit kept going. And to this day, Mr. Dog has been chasing Brer Rabbit, and if you go out in the woods with any dog, as soon as he smells the rabbit's track, he'll bark and tell him to come back.

Dog Tails – Canine Fairy Tales, Myths And Legends

Kulloo, A Faithful Dog

A Tale From Simla - India

This story has been edited and adapted from Alice Elizabeth Dracott's book, Simla Village Tales, first published in 1906 by John Murray, London.

A certain Bunniah or merchant married a woman of his own caste, and they set out to a distant city. On the way he fell ill with a headache, so she sat by the wayside and pressed his head. While doing so a man passed by, and asked for a little fire to light his cheelum for a smoke, but the merchant's wife replied: "I cannot leave my husband, for I am holding his head while he sleeps."

"Put some clothes under his head, and he will sleep," advised the stranger. This she did, but, while giving the fire to the man, he seized her, and, placing her upon his horse, rode away. When the Bunniah awoke, it was to find himself all alone but for his faithful dog Kulloo.

"Master," said Kulloo, "let us become Fakirs, and beg from door to door."

So they set out to beg, and one day came to the house of the robber who had stolen the Bunniah's wife, and she, not recognising her husband or his dog, gave them money and food. But the dog knew her, and that evening he spoke to his master, and asked him if he too had seen his wife. The Bunniah had not, and, guided by Kulloo, he set out to find her.

When they arrived at the robber's house, and made themselves known, the woman was greatly vexed, for the robber was rich, and gave her a very comfortable home, but she pretended to be friendly and invited her husband to dine there that night, telling him that, afterwards, when he had the chance, he could kill the robber.

When the Bunniah had gone, she and the robber arranged a trap for him. It was a hole in the floor, very large and deep, with spikes fixed in the sides of it, so that anybody who fell in might die. Over the hole they set a large brass thalee or plate, so that, while the Bunniah leaned heavily upon it to eat his food, both it and he would fall into the hole.

All happened as they anticipated, and when the poor Bunniah found himself in a deep hole, full of spikes, he thought his last hour had come. But faithful Kulloo came to his rescue, and, taking out the spikes with his teeth, soon set his master free.

The Bunniah then lost no time in seeking the robber, and found him lying fast asleep. so he killed him, and cut off his head, then, taking his wife with him, left the place.

Kulloo followed closely, and licked up each drop of blood which fell from the robber's head, in case it might leave a trace of the deed, and get his master into trouble. He was a wise dog, and knew the woman was wicked, so she hated him, and made up her mind that she would neither eat nor drink until he was dead.

The Bunniah enquired why she would not touch any food, and she told him she would only do so if he killed Kulloo. This the man refused to do, but, after a while, he consented. Poor Kulloo, when he knew his last hour had come, begged his master to bury him carefully, and to see that his head, which the Bunniah meant to cut off, was buried with him, for a time was yet to come when he would again save his master's life.

After Kulloo was dead and buried the wicked woman was happy, and ate and drank as before, but, after a few days, she went and gave notice at the Court that the Bunniah was a cruel robber, who had killed her husband, and stolen her away. The police seized him, and he was taken up for murder; but, just as the Judge was about to pronounce the sentence of death upon him, he remembered faithful Kulloo, and at the same moment the dog appeared!

All were surprised when he stood before the Judge, and asked leave to speak. He then told the whole story of the robber and the wicked woman, and thus, for a second time, saved his master's life, but, having said his say, poor Kulloo disappeared and was never seen again.

The Bear, The Dog, And The Cat

A Russian Tale

This story has been edited and adapted from Aleksander Nikolaevich's book, Russian Folk-Tales, first published in 1915 by Kegan Paul, Trench, Trubner & Co, Ltd.

Once there lived a peasant who had a good dog, and as the dog grew old it left off barking and guarding the yard and the storehouses. Because of this its master would no longer nourish it, so the dog went into the wood and lay under a tree to die.

Then a bear came up and asked him, "Hello, Dog, why are you lying here?"

"I have come to die of hunger. You see how unjust people are. As long as you have any strength, they feed you and give you drink, but when your strength dies away and you become old they drive you from the courtyard."

"Well, Dog, would you like something to eat?"

"I certainly should."

"Well, come with me and I will feed you."

So they went on. On the way a foal met them.

"Look at me," said the bear, and he began to claw the ground with his paws. "Dog, O dog!"

"What do you want?"

"Look, are my eyes beautiful?"

"Yes, Bear, they are beautiful."

So the bear began clawing at the ground more savagely still. "Dog, O dog, is my hair dishevelled?"

"It is dishevelled, Bear."

"Dog, O dog, is my tail raised?"

"Yes, it is raised."

Then the bear laid hold of the foal by the tail, and the foal fell to the ground. The bear tore her to pieces and said, "Well, Dog, eat as much as you will, and when everything is in order, come and see me."

So the dog lived by himself and had no cares, and when he had eaten all and was again hungry, he ran up to the bear.

"Well, my brother, have you done?"

"Yes, I have done, and again I am hungry."

"What! Are you hungry again? Do you know where your old mistress lives?"

"I do."

"Well, then, come. I will steal your mistress's child out of the cradle, and you chase me away and take the child back. Then you may go back and she will go on feeding you, as she formerly did, with bread."

So they agreed, and the bear ran up to the hut and stole the child out of the cradle. The child cried, and the woman burst out. She hunted him, hunted him, but could not catch him. so they came back, and the mother wept, and the other women were afflicted. Then from somewhere or other the dog appeared, and he drove the bear away, took the child and brought it back.

"Look," said the woman, "here is your old dog saving your child!"

So they ran to meet him, and the mother was very glad and joyous. "Now," she said, "I shall never discharge this old dog anymore."

So they took him in, fed him with milk, gave him bread, and asked him only to taste the things. And they told the peasant, "Now you must keep and feed the dog, for he saved my child from the bear, and you were saying he had no strength!"

This all suited the dog very well, and he ate his fill, and he said, "May God grant health to the bear who did not let me die of hunger!" and he became the bear's best friend.

*

Once there was an evening party given at the peasant's house. At that time the bear came in as the dog's guest. "Hail, Dog, How is your luck, these day? Is it bread you are eating?"

"Praise be to God," answered the dog, "it is no mere living, it is butter week. And what are you doing? Let us go into the izbá. The masters have gone out for a walk and will not see what you are doing. Come into the izbá and go and hide under the stove as fast as you can. I will await you there and will call you."

"Very well."

And so they went into the izbá. The dog saw that his master's guests had drunk too much, and made ready to receive his friend. The bear drank up one glass, then another, and broke it. The guests began singing songs, and the bear wanted to chime in. But the dog persuaded him, "Do not sing, it would only do harm."

But it was no good, for he could not keep the bear silent, and he began singing his song. Then the guests heard the noise, laid hold of a stick and began to beat him. He burst out and ran away, and just got away with his life.

Now the peasant also had a cat, which had ceased catching mice, and even playing tricks. Wherever it might crawl it would break something or spill something. The peasant chased the cat out of the house. But the dog saw that it was going to a miserable life without any food, and secretly began bringing it bread and butter and feeding it. Then the mistress looked on, and as soon as she saw this she began beating the dog, beat it hard, very hard, and saying all the time, "Give the cat no beef, nor bread."

Then, three days later, the dog went to the courtyard and saw that the cat was dying of starvation. "What is the matter?" he said.

"I am dying of starvation: I was able to have enough whilst you were feeding me."

"Come with me."

So they went away. The dog went on, until he saw a drove of horses, and he began to scratch the earth with his paws and asked the cat, "Cat, O cat, are my eyes beautiful?"

"No, they are not beautiful."

"Say that they are beautiful!"

So the cat said, "They are beautiful."

"Cat, O cat, is my fur dishevelled?"

"No it is not dishevelled."

"Say, you idiot, that it is dishevelled."

"Well, it is dishevelled."

"Cat, O cat, is my tail raised?"

"No, it is not raised."

"Say, you fool, that it is raised." Then the dog made a dash at a mare, but the mare kicked him back, and the dog died.

So the cat said, "Now I can see that his eyes are very red, and his fur is dishevelled, and his tail is raised. Good-bye, brother Dog, I will go home to die."

Why Dogs Chase Foxes

An Iroquois Tale

This tale has been edited and adapted from Mabel Powers' book, Stories the Iroquois Tell Their Children, published in 1917 by the American Book Company, New York.

A fox was running through the wood near a river. He had a fish in his mouth.

The fish had been stolen from a man who lived down the stream. The fox had been passing near the man's wigwam. He saw the fish hanging by the fire. It was cleaned and ready to cook.

"What a tasty breakfast!" thought the fox. "I think I will watch the man eat."

Soon the man went into the wigwam. The fox slipped up to the fire. He seized the fish, and ran away with it.

When the man came back, he had no breakfast. The fish was gone. No fox was to be seen.

The fox ran along, feeling much pleased with himself.

"What a cunning fox I am," he chuckled. "I will play another foxy trick. This time it shall be on the bear I see coming."

He ran up a tree that had been bent halfway to earth by the West Wind. There he began to eat his fish. He smacked his lips so loudly that the bear heard him.

The bear stopped under the tree, and asked, "What are you eating that tastes so good?"

For answer the fox threw down a bit of the fish. The bear smacked his lips and cried, "More! More!"

"Go to the river, swim out to the big log, and catch your own fish," called the fox. "It's very easy! Just drop your tail into the water. Hold it there till a fish comes along and bites, then pull it up. That is the way I catch my fish. You can catch all the fish you want with your own tail."

The bear hurried on to the river. He swam to the log and dropped his tail into the water, as the fox had advised.

All day he sat and fished with his tail, for bears then had very long tails.

The sun set, but no fish had pulled his tail. All night the bear sat on the log and fished. Cold North Wind blew his breath over the water. The river grew still and white.

Towards morning, the bear felt that his tail was getting very heavy. Now at last he was sure he had a fish. He tried to pull it up. But alas, his tail was frozen fast in the ice.

Then the fox came along. He laughed long and loudly at the bear, and asked if the fishing was good.

Some dogs heard the fox, and came tearing through the thick underbrush. They saw the fox and started after him.

The fox slyly led them on to the frozen river toward the bear. The bear saw them coming, and called to the fox to go around some other way. The fox made believe he did not hear, and came straight on to the bear to ask him what he had said.

The dogs leaped upon the bear. The bear struggled. He gave one great pull, and freed himself from the ice. He struck at the dogs so fiercely with his great paws, that they soon left him, and went on after the fox.

Dogs have been running after foxes ever since.

When the bear got his breath, he stood up and looked around at his tail. He found he had only a small piece left. Most of his tail had been left in the ice.

This is why bears have short tails, and why dogs still love to chase the fox.

The Dog And The Shadow

A Traditional Fable

This story has been adapted from William Patten's version that originally appeared in The Junior Classics, Volume 1, Fairy And Wonder Tales, published in 1912 by P. F. Collier & Son, New York.

A Dog got a piece of meat and was carrying it home in his mouth to eat it in peace. On his way home he had to cross a plank lying across a running brook. As he crossed, he looked down and saw his own shadow reflected in the water. Thinking it was another dog with another piece of meat, he wanted to have that also. So he snapped at the shadow in the water, but as he opened his mouth the piece of meat fell out, dropped into the water and was never seen more.

Dog Tails – Canine Fairy Tales, Myths And Legends

Black Dog Of The Pennine Hills

An English Tale

This tale is my own version of a traditional legend that probably has its roots in early Saxon or Norse storytelling, and shows a common grounding with tales such as Gytrash and The Barghest.

In the rugged hills that form the spine of England, shrouded in mist and mystery, there lurked a fearsome creature known as the Black Dog of the Hanging Hills. With fur as dark as the night sky and eyes that burned like embers, this spectral hound was said to haunt the lonely roads and misty valleys of the region.

Legend had it that the Black Dog was a harbinger of doom, appearing to travellers as an omen of impending tragedy or misfortune. Those who encountered the creature were said to be plagued by ill luck and misfortune, their lives forever marked by the shadow of the Black Dog's presence.

Among the townsfolk who lived near the Hanging Hills was a young farmer named Solomon. Solomon had heard the stories of the Black Dog since he was a boy, but he had never encountered the creature himself. He dismissed the tales as old superstitions, believing them to be nothing more than fanciful legends meant to frighten children.

One moonlit night, as Solomon was returning home from market, he heard a mournful howling echoing through the hills. His heart skipped a beat as he realized it was the sound of the Black Dog, the creature he had dismissed as mere legend.

Fearful yet curious, Solomon followed the eerie howling deeper into the hills, his lantern casting long shadows on the mist-covered ground. As he ventured further from the safety of the village, the howling grew louder, echoing off the ancient stones and gnarled trees.

Suddenly, Solomon stumbled upon a clearing bathed in moonlight, and there, standing before him, was the Black Dog. The creature loomed before him, its eyes gleaming with an otherworldly light, and Solomon felt a chill run down his spine.

But to his surprise, the Black Dog did not attack. Instead, it regarded him with an almost human expression, as if it were trying to communicate something. Solomon felt a sense of empathy for the creature, sensing that it was not the malevolent force that the legends claimed it to be.

With a trembling hand, he reached out to touch the Black Dog, expecting to feel icy fur or cold stone. To his amazement, the creature nuzzled his hand, its touch warm and comforting despite its eerie appearance.

In that moment, Solomon realized that the Black Dog was not a creature of darkness, but a guardian of the hills, watching over the land and its inhabitants with silent vigilance. Moved by compassion, he offered the Black Dog food and shelter, welcoming it into his life with open arms.

From that day forth, Solomon and the Black Dog became unlikely companions, roaming the hills together and sharing in each other's company. And though the townsfolk continued to fear the spectral hound, Solomon knew in his heart that the Black Dog was not a creature to be feared but a loyal guardian and protector of the land.

And so, the legend of the Black Dog of the Pennine Hills lived on, a testament to the power of empathy and understanding in a world where superstition often clouded the truth.

Why A Man Loves His Dog

An Iroquois Tale

This tale has been edited and adapted from Mabel Powers' book, Stories the Iroquois Tell Their Children, published in 1917 by the American Book Company, New York.

The dog is man's best friend. He is the comrade by day and the protector by night. As long as the dog has strength, he will fight for his friend.

The People says this is how the dog came to take his part.

A man and his dogs went into the woods to hunt. It was in the days when dogs and men could talk together, and each understood the language of the other.

When they reached the woods, the dogs began to talk with the man. They told him many wonderful things about the woods, which he did not know. They taught him many tricks of the chase, how to scent and track the game, and where to look for trails.

The man listened to what the dogs said, and he did as they told him. Soon the sledge which the dogs had drawn to the woods was piled high with deer and other game.

Never had the man's arrows brought him so much game. Never had he met with such success in hunting. He was so pleased that he said to the dogs, "I shall always talk with you, give ear to what you say, and be one of you."

"Ah, but listen!" said the dogs. "If you wish to be one of us, you must live under the law of dogs, not men. Animals have laws different from those of men. When two dogs meet for the first time, they try their strength to see which is the better dog.

"Men do not fight when strangers meet, they shake hands. As we fight strange dogs, so you, too, must fight strange men, to see which is the best man, if you are to live under the law of dogs."

The man said he would think it over, and at sunrise give his answer. People always sleep before deciding a question.

Next morning, the man said he would live under the law of animals, and fight strange men.

The following day, the man made ready to leave the woods. From the basswood, he made a strong harness for the dogs, so that they could draw the load of game back to the camp for him.

When the sun was high, the man and the dogs started with the sledge load of game. They had not gone far before they saw two strange people coming.

"Now," said the dogs to the man, "remember you are living under the dog's law. You must fight these strange men."

The man attacked first one stranger and then the other. At last both turned on him, and when they left him, he was nearly dead. At this, the dogs took a hand. They leaped upon the people and drove them from the woods. Then they came back to where their friend lay on the ground, and began to talk with him and lick his face.

The man could not speak for some time, but when his voice came to him, he said to the dogs, "No longer do I wish to live under the law of animals. No more shall I fight strangers. From this time, I shall shake hands with strangers, and bid them welcome. From this time, I shall be a man and live under the law of men."

"Then," said the dogs sadly, "we shall no longer be able to talk with you, and tell you the things that we know. But we will always stand by you. We will be your friends and will fight for you, when you need us as you did today."

This is why a man and his dog are now unable to speak each other's language. This is also why a man's dog will fight to the death for his friend.

*

Not only is the dog a true friend to the people in this world, but in the next as well. It seems that the soul of a man on its journey to the Happy Hunting Ground must cross a deep, swift-running stream. On either side of this dark river, there stand two dogs who hold in their teeth a great log upon which the souls pass.

The soul of a man who has been kind to his dog crosses the log easily, for the dogs stand guard. As the soul of such a man reaches the river, they say, "This man was kind to his dog. He gave him of his own food, and the dog always had a warm place by his fire. We will help this man to cross."

Then the dogs grip the log firmly in their teeth, and hold it steady while the soul of the kind man passes over.

But if the soul of a man who has been unkind to his dog comes to the river, the dogs say, "This man was cruel to his dog. He gave his dog no place by the fire, he beat him, he let him go hungry. This man shall not cross."

Then the dogs grip the log lightly in their teeth, and when the soul of the unkind man is halfway across, they turn it quickly to one side, and the soul is thrown into the deep, dark river.

Many a man has been kind to his dog, that he might make sure of a safe crossing on that log.

The Three Friends, - The Monkey, the Dog, and the Carabao

A Tagalog, Philippines Tale

This story has been adapted from Dean S. Fansler's version that originally appeared in Filipino Popular Tales, published in 1921 by The Folk-lore Society. This story was originally narrated by José M. Hilario, a Tagalog from Batangas.

Once there lived three friends, a monkey, a dog, and a carabao. They were getting tired of city life, so they decided to go to the country to hunt. They took along with them rice, meat, and some kitchen utensils.

The first day the carabao was left at home to cook the food, so that his two companions might have something to eat when they returned from the hunt. After the monkey and the dog had departed, the carabao began to fry the meat. Unfortunately the noise of the frying was heard by the Buñgisñgis in the forest. Seeing this chance to fill his stomach, the Buñgisñgis went up to the carabao, and said, "Well, friend, I see that you have prepared food for me."

For an answer, the carabao made a furious attack on him. The Buñgisñgis was angered by the carabao's lack of hospitality, and, seizing him by the horn, threw him knee-deep into the earth. Then the Buñgisñgis ate up all the food and disappeared.

When the monkey and the dog came home, they saw that everything was in disorder, and found their friend sunk knee-deep in the ground. The carabao informed them that a big strong man had come and beaten him in a fight. The three then cooked their food. The Buñgisñgis saw them cooking, but he did not dare attack all three of them at once, for in union there is strength.

The next day the dog was left behind as cook. As soon as the food was ready, the Buñgisñgis came and spoke to him in the same way he had spoken to the carabao. The dog began to snarl, and the Buñgisñgis, taking offence, threw him down. The dog could not cry to his companions for help, for, if he did, the Buñgisñgis would certainly kill him. So he retired to a corner of the room and watched his unwelcome guest eat all of the food. Soon after the Buñgisñgis's departure, the monkey and the carabao returned. They were angry to learn that the Buñgisñgis had been there again.

The next day the monkey was cook, but, before cooking, he made a pitfall in front of the stove. After putting away enough food for his companions and himself, he put the rice on the stove. When the Buñgisñgis came, the monkey said very politely, "Sir, you have come just in time. The food is ready, and I hope you'll compliment me by accepting it."

The Buñgisñgis gladly accepted the offer, and, after sitting down in a chair, began to devour the food. The monkey took hold of a leg of the chair, gave a jerk, and sent his guest tumbling into the pit. He then filled the pit with earth, so that the Buñgisñgis was buried with no solemnity.

When the monkey's companions arrived, they asked about the Buñgisñgis. At first the monkey was not inclined to tell them what had happened, but, on being urged and urged by them, he finally said that the Buñgisñgis was buried "there in front of the stove." His foolish companions, curious, began to dig up the grave. Unfortunately the Buñgisñgis was still alive. He jumped out, and killed the dog and lamed the carabao, but the monkey climbed up a tree, and so escaped.

One day while the monkey was wandering in the forest, he saw a beehive on top of a vine.

"Now I'll certainly kill you," said someone coming towards the monkey.

Turning around, the monkey saw the Buñgisñgis. "Spare me," he said, "and I will give up my place to you. The king has appointed me to ring that bell up there for each hour of the day," pointing to the top of the vine.

"All right! I accept the position," said the Buñgisñgis.

"Stay here while I find out what time it is," said the monkey. The monkey had been gone a long time, and the Buñgisñgis, becoming impatient, pulled the vine. The bees immediately buzzed about him, and punished him for his curiosity.

Maddened with pain, the Buñgisñgis went in search of the monkey, and found him playing with a boa-constrictor. "You villain! I'll not hear any excuses from you. You shall certainly die," he said.

"Don't kill me, and I will give you this belt which the king has given me," pleaded the monkey.

Now, the Buñgisñgis was pleased with the beautiful colours of the belt, and wanted to possess it, so he said to the monkey, "Put the belt around me, then, and we shall be friends."

The monkey placed the boa-constrictor around the body of the Buñgisñgis. Then he pinched the boa, which soon made an end of his enemy.

The First Lapdog

An Irish Tale

This tale has been adapted from Jane Francesca Agnes Wilde's book, Ancient legends, Mystic Charms & Superstitions of Ireland, published by Chatto And Windus, London in 1919.

In Cormac's Glossary there is an interesting account of how the first lapdog came into Ireland, for the men of Britain were under strict orders that no lapdog should be given to the Gael, either of solicitation or of free will, for gratitude or friendship.

Now it happened that Cairbré Musc went to visit a friend of his in Britain, who made him right welcome and offered him everything he possessed, save only his lapdog, for that was forbidden by the law. Yet this beautiful lapdog was the only possession that Cairbré coveted, and he laid his plans cunningly to obtain it.

There was a law at that time in Britain to this effect: "Every criminal shall be given as a forfeit for his crime to the person he has injured."

Now Cairbré had a wonderful dagger, around the haft of which was an adornment of silver and gold. It was a precious jewel, and he took fat meat and rubbed it all over the haft, with much grease. Then he set it before the lapdog, who began to gnaw at the haft, and continued gnawing all night till the morning, so that the haft was spoiled and was no longer beautiful.

Then on the morrow, Cairbré made complaint that his beautiful dagger was destroyed, and he demanded a just recompense.

"That is indeed fair," said his friend, "I shall pay a price for the trespass."

"I ask no other price," said Cairbré, "than what the law of Britain allows me, namely, the criminal for his crime."

So the lapdog was given to Cairbré, and it was called ever after *Mug-Eimé*, the slave of the haft, which name clung to it because it passed into servitude as a forfeit for the trespass.

Now when Cairbré brought it back to Erin with him, all the kings of Ireland began to wrangle and contend for possession of the lapdog, and the contention at last ended this way: It was agreed that the dog should abide for a certain time in the house of each king. Afterwards the dog littered, and each of them had a pup of the litter, and from this stock descends every lapdog in Ireland from that time till now.

After a long while the lapdog died, and the bare skull being brought to the blind poet Maer to try his power of divination, he at once exclaimed, through the prophetic power and vision in him, "O Mug-Eimé, this is indeed the head of Mug-Eimé, the slave of the haft, that was brought into Ireland and given over to the fate of a bondsman, and to the punishment of servitude as a forfeit."

The Word Hound

An Irish Tale

This tale has been adapted from Jane Francesca Agnes Wilde's book, Ancient legends, Mystic Charms & Superstitions of Ireland, published by Chatto And Windus, London in 1919.

The word hound entered into many combinations as a name for various animals. Thus the rabbit was called, "the hound of the brake." The hare was called the "brown hound", while the moth was called "the hound of fur," owing to the voracity with which it devoured raiment. And the otter is still called by the Irish *Madradh-Uisgue* (the dog of the water).

The names of most creatures of the animal kingdom were primitive, the result evidently of observation. Thus the hedgehog was named "the ugly little fellow." The ant was the "slender one." The trout, *Breac*, or "the spotted," from the skin. And the wren was called "the Druid bird," because if anyone understood the chirrup, they would have a knowledge of coming events as foretold by the bird.

About the Editor

Born in 1962 into a household that lived and breathed sports, the editor's dad was a seasoned senior amateur and lower league professional footballer. Not just that, he managed his own businesses in cahoots with Clive's mum, who was no slouch either – she was a skilled and award-winning dancer.

After snagging a degree in History from Leeds University, our storyteller took a rather serendipitous stroll into the burgeoning world of information technology in the late '80s. Like father, like son, they say. Alongside a flourishing tech career, Clive dabbled in various writing and acting pursuits, from freelancing as a journalist and book reviewer (with a coveted by-line in The Sunday People) to gracing stages in village halls and even professional theatres all across the south of the UK for a good decade.

In a nod to the family's sporting legacy, Clive - long after hanging up his own boots - delved into the world of live TV broadcasts. Armed with a wealth of rugby knowledge, he became one of the go-to 'statos' for the BBC, ITV, TVNZ, and EuroSport, covering everything from Heineken Cups to Six Nations, World Sevens, and World Cups in the late '90s.

For a deeper dive into this fascinating journey, head over to clivegilson.com.

Dog Tails – Canine Fairy Tales, Myths And Legends

ORIGINAL FICTION BY CLIVE GILSON

- *Songs of Bliss*
- *Out of the Walled Garden*
- *The Mechanic's Curse*
- *The Insomniac Booth*
- *A Solitude of Stars*

AS EDITOR – *FIRESIDE TALES*

- **Wales** - *Tales From the Land of Dragons*
- **Scotland** - *Tales From the Land of The Brave*
- **Ireland** - *Tales From the Land of Saints And Scholars*
- **England** - *Tales From the Land of Hope And Glory*
- **France** - *Tales from Gallia*
- **Germany** - *Tales from Germania*
- **Scandinavia** - *Tales From Lands of Snow and Ice*
- **Scandinavia** - *Tales From the Viking Isles*
- **Finland** - *Tales From the Forest Lands*
- **Scandinavia** - *Tales From the Old Norse*
- **Spain & Portugal** - *Tales From the Land of Rabbits*
- **Italy** - *Tales Told by Bulls and Wolves*
- **Greece** - *Tales of Fire and Bronze*
- **The Balkans** - *Tales From the Samodivi*
- **Romania** - *Tales From the Land of the Strigoi*
- **Hungary** - *Tales Told by the Wind Mother*
- **First Nations** - *Okaraxta - Tales from The Great Plains*
- **First Nations** - *Tibik-Kìzis – Tales from The Great Lakes & Canada*
- **First Nations** - *Jóhonaa'éí –Tales from America's Southwest*
- **First Nations** - *Qugaaĝix̂ - Tales from Alaska & The Arctic*
- **First Nations** - *Karahkwa - Tales from America's Eastern States*
- **USA** - *Pot-Likker - Tales and Settler Stories from America*
- **West Africa** - *Arokin Tales*
- **East Africa** – *Hadithi Tales*

Dog Tails – Canine Fairy Tales, Myths And Legends

- **Southern Africa** - *Inkathaso Tales*
- **Northern Africa** - *Tarubadur Tales*
- **Central Africa** - *Elephant And Frog*
- **Turkey** - *Tales From The Meddahs*
- **The Arabic diaspora** - *Tales From The Hakawati*
- **Jewish & Armenia** - *Tales Told By Balebos & Gusan*
- **India** – *Tales Told By The Kathaakaar*
- **China** - *Tales Of The Gùshì Yuán*

Milton Keynes UK
Ingram Content Group UK Ltd.
UKHW031040230724
445880UK00007B/72/J